Co-Living Cash Flow:
A BiggerPockets Guide

Co-Living Cash Flow

A BiggerPockets Guide

with Miller McSwain

BiggerPockets
PUBLISHING
Denver, Colorado

Co-Living Cash Flow: A BiggerPockets Guide
Miller McSwain

Published by BiggerPockets Publishing LLC, Denver, CO
Copyright © 2025 by Miller McSwain
All rights reserved.

Publisher's Cataloging-in-Publication Data
Names: McSwain, Miller, 1998-, author.
Title: Co-living cash flow : a BiggerPockets guide / Miller McSwain.
Description: Includes bibliographical references. | Denver, CO: BiggerPockets Publishing LLC, 2025.
Identifiers: LCCN: 2025931116 | ISBN 9781960178879 (hardcover) | 9781960178886 (ebook)
Subjects: LCSH Real estate investment. | Real estate management. | Rental housing--Management. | Home ownership. | Investing. | Personal finance. | BISAC BUSINESS & ECONOMICS / Investments & Securities / Real Estate | BUSINESS & ECONOMICS / Real Estate / General | BUSINESS & ECONOMICS / Personal Finance / Investing
Classification: LCC HD1382.5 .M37 2025 | DDC 332.63/24--dc23

BiggerPockets Guide
Mission Statement

Revolutionize your investing journey with BiggerPockets Guides: a series of laser-focused, in-depth strategy blueprints designed to help you master crucial real estate topics. These books tackle advanced investing subjects head-on, providing you with trustworthy insights that will supercharge your real estate journey.

Say goodbye to expensive guru courses and flashy masterminds. BiggerPockets Guides are your *affordable* ticket to real estate success. We've distilled the valuable knowledge of real experts into accessible guides that connect you with even more free tools and resources on the BiggerPockets website.

Whether you're a seasoned pro or just starting out, our guides will be your secret weapon in helping you navigate the lucrative world of real estate investing with confidence. Get ready to transform your financial future—one guide at a time!

Prepare to Discover...

...the emerging co-living real estate investment strategy, a model that transforms traditional residential properties into community-focused living spaces.

In this guide, you'll learn how to:

- Find properties for co-living success
- Analyze deals to ensure maximum cash flow and long-term profitability
- Design and remodel your properties to attract high-quality residents
- Manage your co-living spaces with ease, from lease agreements to conflict resolution
- Scale your portfolio with tools and systems

Table of Contents

Part I

Introduction

Chapter 1

What Is Co-Living, and How Can It Change Your Life?

Let's play a game. I'm going to try to describe you. Let's see if I hit the mark.

You are looking for the financial freedom you've heard real estate can provide, meaning you have enough cash flow to cover your personal expenses. You could reduce the time you spend at your job so you can spend time doing what you want. You've been researching ways to provide these freedoms by listening to real estate podcasts, reading books, and watching YouTube videos, but most of the "deals" you analyze don't produce life-changing cash flow or they give negative returns.

You are frustrated because people keep telling you that real estate is the best way to build wealth and become free, but they bought their properties years ago and are unaware of how hard it is to find profitable deals these days.

If this sounds like you, you'll greatly benefit from the strategy I teach in this book.

What Is Co-Living?

Co-living is short for community living. It is a rental property strategy in which private rooms are rented to individuals, while common spaces such as the kitchen, living room, and laundry room are shared.

There is a significant emphasis on fostering community, encouraging residents to mingle and make friends rather than stay siloed in their rooms. This is what separates this strategy from the slumlord stigma that surrounds room rentals and boarding houses.

By providing these shared community experiences, affordable housing is created. In most cities around the U.S., studio and one-bedroom apartments are too expensive compared to the salary of a lower-income worker. By providing rooms for rent, a more affordable rental product is introduced into the market that helps this demographic have leftover funds to spend, save, and invest meaningfully, improving their financial health.

History

For thousands of years, people have rented rooms, rather than entire properties, to live more affordably. In the 1800s, boarding houses became popular in the United States as rural workers left their families and moved to urban centers for employment. They often sought affordability over luxury, so they rented individual rooms. This continued to be a popular form of housing well into the 1900s.

Even today, remnants of community living inspired by these early boarding houses remain. College dorm rooms, for example, are occupied by a few students and provide shared living rooms and kitchens. Beyond the dorms, rooms throughout college towns are rented to students by landlords just like you and me. Additionally, resort towns commonly have many room rentals for local workers who cannot afford their own apartment or house.

Shared housing has become less popular since its peak in the 1800s and early 1900s, but it has recently reemerged in the United States. With the rise of the sharing economy, led by companies like Airbnb and Uber, sharing resources like housing has been normalized in mainstream culture. The recent popularization of room rentals has further been driven by rising rental unaffordability and increased density in urban areas.

Advantages

Co-living is truly a win-win for all parties involved. Investors receive benefits that other rental strategies cannot offer, and residents see benefits that no other rental product can provide.

FOR INVESTORS

The first benefit for investors is increased income. Co-living properties typically produce two to three times the income compared to traditional long-term rentals. My co-living houses bring in about $6,000/month, while Zillow estimates they would usually rent for around $2,500/month. The expenses are higher, but the resulting cash flow is leagues ahead of long-term rentals.

Second, co-living properties have low vacancy risk. In a six-bedroom house, you have six different sources of income. If one resident leaves, you are still collecting the majority of the rent. Additionally, each resident likely works for a different company, so you reduce the risk that a company or industry goes under and you lose all of your income.

Third, you can feel good about your positive impact on your residents by providing affordable, community-focused housing.

FOR RESIDENTS

The first benefit for residents is the affordability of rooms compared to traditional options. Studio and one-bedroom apartments are the cheapest options in most cities, but even these can be too expensive for many locals. By providing a more affordable option, many residents can lead a financially healthy life that would be difficult or impossible otherwise.

Second, they get access to a community. Having a built-in community is a huge benefit, especially since many residents are new to town. Alternatively, if they move into an apartment, they may see their neighbors occasionally but are unlikely to develop friendships as easily as in a co-living property.

Third, co-living properties provide many conveniences. Rather than having to stock a kitchen and living room with furniture and appliances, all furnishings are provided, and a housekeeper maintains these spaces. Shared supplies such as toilet paper, paper towels, trash bags, dish soap, and more are included, reducing residents' expenses. We will also discuss many other conveniences throughout the book, but these are some of the most important ones.

Challenges

Co-living isn't a perfect strategy. While it offers many benefits, it also comes with its share of disadvantages.

FOR INVESTORS

For investors, co-living has much higher management needs than other strategies. With many people sharing a house, resident conflicts sometimes require intervention.

Turnovers are much more common, as co-living residents often stay for shorter periods than traditional tenants. In addition, you'll have many leases at a single property rather than a family on a single lease. The sheer number of leases means you'll spend more time keeping all the rooms occupied.

Lastly, co-living properties experience higher wear and tear and thus require repairs and maintenance more often. This costs both money and time to communicate with the residents about the issues and schedule a contractor to make the repairs.

FOR RESIDENTS

There are challenges for the residents too. There will be compatibility issues with at least some housemates, as personalities may conflict. I will present tactics that can ease the friction, but inevitably, there will be some issues. For example, one resident might be incapable of socializing until after their morning coffee. Another resident may be bubbly, skipping into the kitchen, ready for morning conversation. This can be challenging for the first resident, as they sometimes wish they were left alone to drink their coffee in peace.

Tension between residents can arise due to differing standards for cleanliness. Some may leave their shoes on as they walk through the house, tracking dirt along with them. Others may see this and become frustrated because they always take their shoes off at the door. While the housekeeper will help with cleanliness issues, there are times when residents confront each other and discuss solutions on their own.

Lastly, residents must abide by house rules. They know rules are needed for the good of the house, but they can find policies for guests, quiet hours, and pets to be restrictive.

Why Now?

Room rentals have existed for thousands of years, but what makes co-living a great cash-flow strategy today? And with all the other strategies you could implement to produce cash flow, can you trust the co-living strategy to be a great option for you well into the future?

Rental Unaffordability

Rental unaffordability measures how difficult it is for someone to pay their monthly rent. It is based on their income and the cost of rent.

$$\text{Rental Unaffordability} = \frac{\text{Annual Rent}}{\text{Annual Income}}$$

For example, someone who makes $60,000/year and pays $16,800/year ($1,400/month) in rent has an unaffordability of 28 percent. This is pretty good! Personal finance experts advise that you spend 30 percent or less of your income on housing to be financially healthy.[1] This leaves you with 70 percent of your income to pay for transportation, groceries, and fun, and still have some left to save/invest.

---

[1] Laura McMullen, "How Much Should I Spend on Rent?" NerdWallet, December 9, 2024, https://www.nerdwallet.com/article/finance/how-much-should-i-spend-on-rent.

If you watch the same news I do, you've probably heard that people's pockets are getting lighter, and rent is becoming unaffordable. As shown in Figure 1, rental unaffordability is well over the recommended 30 percent threshold for the average worker and is only getting worse. While rentals are unaffordable for the average worker in the average city, it is even worse for those in more expensive cities.

Average Worker – Rental Unaffordability

— Rental Unaffordability   ···Trendline   — — Affordable Threshold

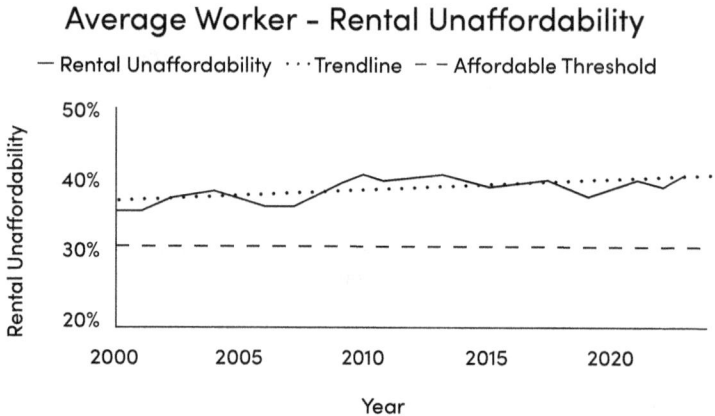

Figure 1. Average worker—rental unaffordability. Income from St. Louis FRED; rent from iPropertyManagement

The situation changes, however, for lower-income workers. I will discuss other resident demographics that room rentals cater to in later parts of the book, but this is the largest demographic, so I'll focus on them for this argument.

In 2023, the median income for an individual was $42,220/year, according to St. Louis FRED.[2] Based on data from the U.S. Department of Labor, the average full-time minimum wage income for 2023 was $21,500/year, or about 51 percent of the average individual's income.[3]

Additionally, lower-income workers often seek to rent a one-bedroom apartment, as the average-sized home strains their budget,

[2]   "Median Personal Income in the United States," FRED: Federal Reserve Bank of St. Louis, updated September 10, 2024, https://fred.stlouisfed.org/series/MEPAINUSA646N.

[3]   "Changes in Basic Minimum Wages in Non-Farm Employment Under State Law: Selected Years 1968 to 2024," U.S. Department of Labor, accessed January 15, 2025, https://www.dol.gov/agencies/whd/state/minimum-wage/history.

and one-bedroom apartments are their cheapest options. Based on Apartment List's data from 2017 to 2024, a one-bedroom apartment usually rents for around 88 percent of the average rental.[4]

Based on these two assumptions, Figure 2 shows the unaffordability of lower-income workers who rent a one-bedroom apartment. Lower-income workers have to spend roughly 70 percent of their income on rent and thus are in financial jeopardy. This leaves little room for personal spending and saving without going into debt. Something needs to change if these individuals are to improve their financial position.

Lower-Income Worker – Rental Unaffordability

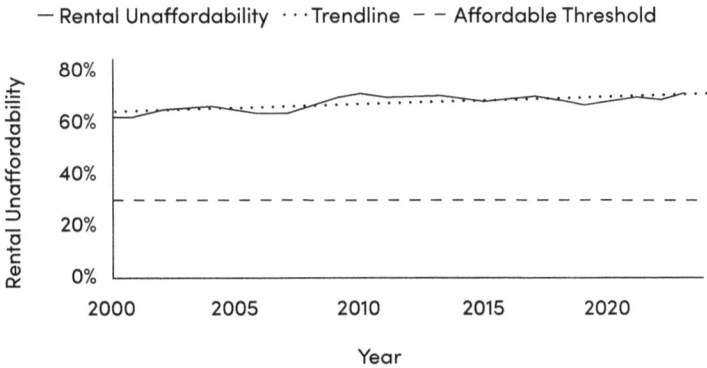

Figure 2. Lower-income worker—rental unaffordability. Income from St. Louis FRED and modified; rent from iPropertyManagement and modified

There are three ways to fix this unaffordability issue for lower-income workers, some of them more realistic than others.

First, a significant rise in their income could make things more affordable. However, as you can see in Figure 3, even if rents hold constant and incomes continue to rise at their same pace since 2000, the affordability threshold wouldn't be reached for seventy years! I knew the gap was significant, but I was shocked when I plotted this data. While this is technically a solution to the problem, it is doubtful, as rents will not be held constant. In reality, they will continue rising over time, keeping the gap constant or widening it.

---

4   "Apartment List National Rent Report," Apartment List, March 2, 2025, https://www.apartmentlist.com/research/national-rent-data.

Rising Income - Unaffordability Solution

— Actual Annual Income　···Projected Annual Income　− −Affordable Threshold

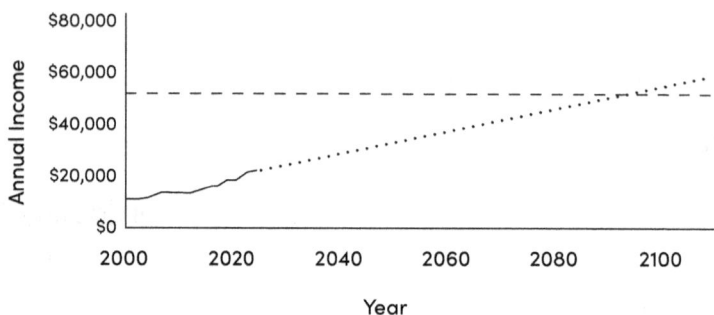

Figure 3. Rising income—unaffordability solution. Income from St. Louis FRED, modified, and extrapolated

Another potential way to make rental unaffordability more reasonable is for rents to decrease.

In Figure 4, I assumed that income was held constant while rent decreased at 5 percent per year. Even in this case, the affordability threshold wouldn't be reached for sixteen years. In reality, it is very unlikely that rent will decrease for even a single year, let alone sixteen years. Data from the Federal Reserve Bank of St. Louis shows that rent has not decreased at all since the Great Depression. Also, 5 percent drops are very extreme and used to prove the point. If rents were to ever drop, it would likely be by much less. Decreasing rents is technically a solution; however, it is doubtful.

Decreasing Rent - Unaffordability Solution

— Actual 1 BR Apartment Rent ⋯ Projected 1 BR Apartment Rent
− − Affordable Threshold

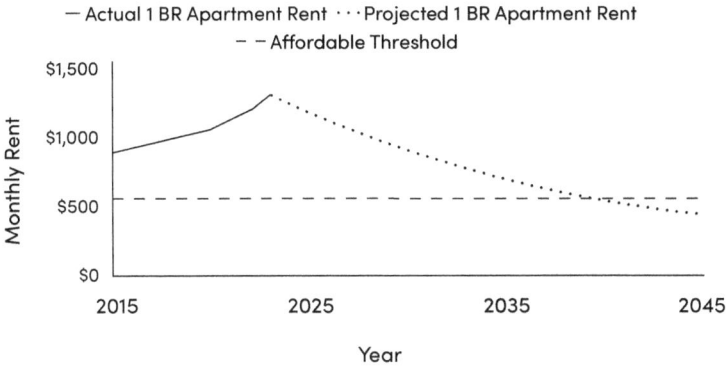

Figure 4. Rent from iPropertyManagement and modified

The third and only realistic solution is offering lower-income workers a drastically cheaper housing product they can comfortably afford on their current income. What is this product, you ask? It is a room in a shared house!

I mentioned earlier that in 2023, the average lower-income worker in the United States earned $21,500/year. To be financially healthy, they need to spend 30 percent of this income on rent, which means their rent needs to be around $540/month. That is a very standard room rental price, and not by coincidence! Our capitalist financial system saw a demand for cheaper housing for this demographic, and around $540/month is a price that the market supports.

Based on the data for these three scenarios, a cheaper rental product is the only solution to keep the lower-income worker healthy and financially sustained, now and in the future. While there are efforts to build lower-cost housing, many of these attempts have failed, as the price to build has not proven cost-effective for builders, and (since costs are passed on to the end user) the rent is not cheap enough for the resident. Room rentals are a realistic solution, as properties do not need to be built, and government intervention/subsidies do not need to be involved. It is simply employing a house that currently exists for a higher and better use to benefit the investor and the residents that call it home.

Legal Support

I am not the only one who believes that room rentals can solve rental affordability issues; legislators have also supported this solution.

In 2021, Washington and Oregon enacted policies that removed occupancy limits for many properties across the entire state, allowing more unrelated people to live in a house together. Colorado followed their lead in 2024 with a similar policy. Many cities have removed occupancy limits too, with more becoming co-living friendly every month.

When I talk with investors about this strategy, one of the first things they mention is legal risk. With almost all large cities around the United States enacting policies restricting short-term rentals, it is understandable that they are worried that co-living is illegal or will become illegal soon. I don't foresee this happening since co-living and short-term rentals are quite different in the eyes of legislators.

Short-term rentals turn existing long-term rental homes into vacation homes with short-term stays for tourists. The conversion of houses intended for long-term families decreases the rental supply, thus increasing the rents for locals. Co-living, by contrast, converts housing that provides for one family into housing that provides for many more people, reducing the cost of rent for those individuals. Legislators want what is best for their people—or if nothing else, they want to make their people happy and get reelected. Providing cheaper housing is certainly a great way to do that.

Some people have negative associations with shared housing, and for good reason. They probably think of slumlords cramming people into houses like sardines to make a quick buck. This has happened in the past and continues to happen today. The majority of this book, however, focuses on providing top-quality housing that is not a compromise for the residents but an enhanced experience with exceptional service compared to traditional forms of housing. I encourage you to exemplify a landlord who provides this high-quality housing so your neighborhoods, cities, and states see the benefits and continue to support it.

Rocket Scientist to Real Estate Investor

Before diving headfirst into the co-living strategy, let me tell you a story of how I bought six properties within two years, rented all forty-one rooms, and used the cash flow to quit my job!

Discovering Real Estate

Before discovering co-living, I worked as a nuclear rocket scientist—my dream job. I spent high school and college working hard to get excellent grades so I could enter the job field I desired.

Eventually, I was accepted for an internship at NASA after applying many times. While it was prestigious and what I had wanted for so long, within a few weeks, I found that I didn't enjoy the work. I thought I might enjoy a different position more, so I pivoted to another division. Still, I found myself unfulfilled.

After much pondering, I realized I simply did not enjoy working for someone else, no matter what the job was! Sound familiar?

I knew that working a W-2 job would be a means to an end. I needed more freedom than a job could provide—the freedom to build something that was mine, have unlimited income potential, and choose my schedule and direction. Then, I rediscovered rental properties.

Growing up, my parents owned a few rentals and were the classic mom-and-pop landlords. They'd buy a property, fix it themselves, answer the midnight phone calls for maintenance, and dump all the cash flow back into the loan to have a paid-off portfolio before retirement. I was aware of the benefits of property ownership as we'd talk about it sometimes, but I wasn't super interested during the early stages of my life.

At one point, my parents told me they'd help buy me a duplex when I went to college, and I'd manage it while living there. I remembered this promise when I had my realization that I wasn't built to work for someone else.

I was sitting in an apartment when this hit me. How could I self-manage a property? I would just have to roll up my sleeves and figure it out.

After some YouTube searches about how to invest in real estate, I found BiggerPockets. Like many of you, I fell down the rabbit hole and obsessively consumed the content.

While studying real estate, I continued my schooling, mainly on the side, because I knew it wasn't my real passion. Eventually, I graduated, got married, started my career, and my wife and I bought our first property—a single-family home in Colorado—all in a thirty-day span!

Building Our Portfolio

As any young couple consumed by real estate education would do, we decided to house hack our first property (live in one part of the property while renting the rest), and we rented the three extra bedrooms to other young professionals. We were finally real estate investors!

As a nuclear rocket scientist, my brain is wired to think in systems. How can I improve this process? What is the best order to perform these steps? Can I automate this?

Whenever I listed a room, handled a maintenance issue, or processed a move-out, I thought of questions like these and continually improved the checklists, systems, and processes that ran the investment.

Fast-forward one year, and my wife and I had bought our second property: another house hack that we rented by the room. At this point, my systems had been refined and proven to be effective, so I felt I was ready to grow faster. I started partnering with investors who were interested in our business model, and as of the writing of this book, we now have six properties and forty-one rooms! These six properties have allowed us to live for free and generate $8,000/month in cash flow.

This cash flow has allowed me to quit my job as a nuclear rocket scientist and focus all my energy on building our business. As I write this introduction, my wife and I are in Italy celebrating my "retirement" and the life we built with real estate.

Cheers to you for opening this book and taking the first step toward gaining the freedom co-living has provided me. I hope to see you on the other side soon!

Figure 5. Celebration in Amalfi, Italy

What to Expect

I know many folks who have rented rooms in their house, and you might too. But few have taken it a step further and done it at scale. Why not? Because the management is challenging, and there hasn't been a playbook.

Right now, the room rental space is similar to the early days of short-term rentals. Few software programs have been built for this purpose, there aren't many places to learn about it online, and no books have been written about it (until now). It hasn't been a viable option for investors who don't want to invent every piece of the strategy from the ground up.

Well, buckle up! In this book, you'll find the proven solutions and practices I've uncovered in my journey or learned from other investors who have pioneered the space alongside me. By the end, you will know exactly how to run a highly profitable room rental investment business.

It's not rocket science; it's just real estate.

Chapter 2

Enhanced Cash Flow Strategy Comparisons (LTR, STR, MTR, Co-Living)

I
f you are considering the co-living strategy, you might also be considering other real estate strategies that offer increased cash flow compared to traditional long-term rentals (LTR). I like to call any rental strategy that provides more cash flow an enhanced cash-flow strategy. I group co-living rentals with mid-term rentals (MTR) and short-term rentals (STR).

In Figure 6, you can see the annual revenue trends for LTR, MTR, STR, and co-living properties. To keep things apples to apples, in this comparison, I'm assuming a five-bedroom, single-family house purchased in Colorado Springs for each strategy. The results can vary based on the market, though. For example, an STR will likely outperform co-living in a vacation market; however, this comparison represents a typical metro market.

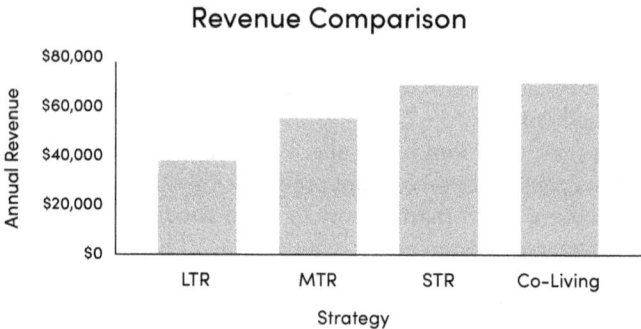

Figure 6. Revenue Comparison[5]

---

[5]   "Rental Market Trends in Colorado Springs, Co," Apartments.com, https://www.apartments.com/rent-market-trends/colorado-springs-co/; "Mid-Term Rentals 101: Learn All About This Rental Type and Why You Should Consider Investing in Them," Furnished Finder, May 17, 2024, https://www.furnishedfinder.com/blog/why-mid-term-rentals; "Colorado Springs, CO Airbnb Market Data," Rabbu, https://rabbu.com/airbnb-data/colorado-springs-co; author's own portfolio data.

Long-Term Rentals

When I refer to long-term rentals, I'm referring to renting out a single-family house to one family for a year or longer. These types of rentals produce the lowest revenue in the group.

The nice thing about LTRs is that the income is very steady. Since tenants are on long-term leases, they'll pay the same monthly amount for the duration of the agreement, no matter the time of year; however, income can have large dips intermittently when extensive repairs are needed, so reserves are essential.

For long-term rentals, management is the least intensive of all the categories we're comapring. Tenants of single-family homes often stay for years at a time, so the time and expenses associated with turnovers are less. Outside of turnovers, you'll also be making maintenance repairs as needed and collecting rent to pay the bills.

Mid-Term Rentals

Mid-term rentals are in the middle of the pack in this comparison. They offer more revenue than LTRs and less than STRs and co-living.

The cash flow is not steady year-round like for an LTR. Instead, there are seasons where you'll make the majority of your income and seasons where you'll make less income, and you may resort to dipping into reserves. This is because MTR tenants are on monthly leases. For example, a tenant may stay for three months at a time of year with higher demand. Since there is higher demand, you can charge more for rent. On the other hand, when a tenant comes to stay for three months in a time of year with lower demand, you'll have to accept a lower rent amount.

MTRs require more management than LTRs. As the name suggests, tenants may stay for one to six months, leading to higher turnover. Also, mid-term properties are fully furnished, so in addition to standard repairs and maintenance, expect to replace or repair the provided furnishings.

Short-Term Rentals

Short-term rentals are among the highest revenue producers. With STRs, you'll have more expenses than with LTRs and MTRs: cleaning, house supplies, utilities, etc.

STRs are highly seasonal, meaning you will experience volatile income fluctuations throughout the year. This is sustainable if you diligently use your cash flow to fill your reserves, as they may be needed during slower seasons.

If you are seeking high cash flow, STRs are a great option, but investigate the legality. Over the last few years, STRs have become highly regulated in urban markets, as they have become popular among investors. An influx of STRs in a market often causes local rents to increase because the local housing supply is converted into accommodations for tourists and other transient renters. I expect local governments will further restrict STRs to fight these rising rents.

STRs require some of the highest management intensity. With STRs, you could have new guests moving in every few days, requiring constant marketing of the space, answering questions, and facilitating move-ins and move-outs. As a hospitality business, you are expected to provide an incredible experience by fixing any issues immediately and providing information about local attractions.

STRs are very competitive, so you must offer premium amenities and furnishings to obtain interest. You may also feel more pressure to improve your property often to stay at the top of the listing services and provide a much better experience than the competition.

Poor management of STRs has extreme consequences. These properties are highly sensitive to reviews, which can help or hurt cash flow. Most STRs are listed on Airbnb or similar platforms, where users rely on reviews to describe the experience and quality of the property. If you are among the best in the market, this can work to your advantage, while being average will produce mediocre results.

Co-Living Rentals
Co-living is effectively tied with STRs for the highest income-producing strategy. With co-living, you'll incur higher expenses, similar to STRs, as you'll likely pay for utilities, cleanings, shared supplies, etc.

In contrast to STRs, co-living produces steadier cash flow as it often caters to longer-term residents who stay for six months or longer. Additionally, co-living income is diversified, as it comes from many different individuals who have different income sources. So if a resident loses their job and doesn't pay rent, or if a resident chooses to leave, you'll still collect the majority of your rent, rarely seeing large dips.

Legally, it is much more likely for co-living to be unregulated than STRs, as co-living helps reduce the cost of housing for locals. There can be limits, however, on the number of people allowed to live in a house together. We will talk about this in Chapter 3 when I discuss occupancy laws.

Co-living has a high level of management, similar to STRs, but in a different way. In the beginning, you will spend a lot of time filling all your vacancies. Once they are filled, those residents often stay for six to twelve months. Going forward, you will have to fill new vacancies as needed, but less frequently than in an STR.

Other than finding residents, you'll find that most of the management is related to the community. You must order shared supplies to the house as needed, mediate resident disputes, and create a positive tenant community through group events and activities. Due to the increased number of occupants, you'll have more repairs and maintenance than LTRs and MTRs, on par with STRs.

Co-living is less sensitive to reviews and is more reliant on the quality of the experience. If the experience is poor at an STR, you may get a three-star review, but you'll probably still collect all the promised rent. If you provide a terrible experience in a co-living property, that resident will leave as soon as their lease term expires, causing you to look for a replacement and lose rent. Conversely, if you provide an outstanding experience, residents will stay with you much longer, reducing turnover and boosting cash flow.

Selecting Your Strategy

Is co-living the best strategy? I'd like to say so, but it depends on your circumstances. When choosing your strategy, consider whether any of them fire you up. Do you like the idea of setting up furnished spaces and renting to transient professionals who are in town for short assignments? If so, MTRs might be best for you. Do you love interior design and desire to provide an exceptional experience for families on vacation? If so, STRs might be a contender. Do you enjoy building community and connecting people? If so, co-living could be a good option.

Next, consider how much time you can devote to the strategy, especially in the beginning. Learning and effectively implementing a new approach can take hundreds of hours. Even after you've become a master, you'll still spend time managing the asset and potentially managing the residents. While some tasks, like property management, can be hired out at some point, there is always a time commitment, and it is usually higher for strategies that produce more income.

Lastly, consider what your cash flow needs are. If you need to quit your job and produce income to live on, you'll likely lean toward STRs or co-living. If you are content with your financial situation and don't need immediate cash flow, MTRs or LTRs may be the best option.

Lastly, you don't have to be exclusive to one strategy; you can mix and match! While I wouldn't recommend learning two strategies simultaneously, adding another strategy to your tool belt could be a good idea once you have mastered another. Two of my co-living properties have fully furnished basements that I rent as MTRs. I'd rather keep things simple and only rent rooms; however, these basements were better used as MTRs rather than two tiny bedrooms due to their size.

Part II

Buying a Co-Living Property

Chapter 3

Selecting a Market

"Location, location, location." Most of you have heard this old real estate adage that still rings true and is applicable to numerous scenarios. At the lowest level, your property's neighborhood influences the proximity to amenities, the general safety of the area, and the type of residents that will be attracted to your property. The city where your property is located determines the jobs your residents may have, policies that help or hurt population growth, and the laws that are applied to your property. The state your property is located in will have more rules and different tax and insurance burdens. Considering where to purchase a co-living property may seem overwhelming, especially if you're looking in the United States. There are fifty unique states, thousands of cities, and hundreds of neighborhoods in each city to choose from. However, by taking a step-by-step approach, you can select the ideal market for your co-living property. (Note: I'll be discussing investing in the U.S. from here out, but you can definitely apply the co-living strategy in other countries. Just make sure to check your local regulations to invest legally!)

Invest Locally or Remotely

One of the first questions to ponder when deciding on a market is whether to invest in your local market or a more distant one. I'll provide the benefits of each, but it is essential to know that investing locally doesn't mean you have to be in the trenches fixing toilets forever.

The goal should always be to operate as if you cannot drive to your property in an emergency. After all, your presence shouldn't be a requirement for your investment, since you may not live in the city forever. In the beginning, I did most of the work myself while documenting the processes, knowing that someone else would run the process in the future. Once I scaled enough, doing all this myself was compromising growth, so I started hiring tasks out. I didn't outsource all the work overnight; it took over a year to get enough cash flow to cover the extra cost. Fortunately, since I spent my time documenting the processes, it was straightforward to hand off the checklists to my new, competent team members. Even though I live less than a ten-minute drive from most of my properties, I never visit them to fix toilets or clean the shared spaces. Instead, I've hired others to perform those low-cost tasks and focused on scaling my portfolio. I'd encourage you to keep this goal in mind, whether you decide to invest in your backyard or not.

Investing Locally

The most significant advantage to investing locally is that it enables you to house hack. Many investors confuse the term "house hacking" with co-living. House hacking is when you live in your property while renting a portion. That portion can be rented in many ways: short-term rental, mid-term rental, garage space, storage sheds, or co-living. In the case of co-living, this often means you are occupying one of the rooms while renting out the other rooms.

My wife and I house hacked our first property! We purchased a house with three bedrooms on the main level and two bedrooms in the basement. We saw how having roommates would supercharge our journey to financial freedom, so we dove in and rented the rooms. Depending on how comfortable you want to be vs. how much income you want to produce, you can slice a co-living house hack in many ways. In our first property, we could have stayed in one room and rented out the other four, occupied the entire main level while renting the basement, or occupied the entire downstairs while renting the main level.

To balance comfort and income potential, we opted to occupy the two rooms in the basement while renting the three rooms on the main level. We also installed a locking door between the two levels and a kitchenette in the basement. With those two improvements, we essentially created our own private apartment. The best part was that it was larger than the college apartment we had moved from, and it cost less because the roommates paid 80 percent of our mortgage payment for us. Since the alternative was renting a small, more expensive apartment or occupying this large house alone, house hacking was a no-brainer that allowed us to learn the co-living ropes with little risk.

If you or your partner don't want to live with housemates, the co-living strategy is still fantastic for purchasing non-owner-occupied properties.

Whether you live in the property or not, investing locally can be great for investors with more time than money. Living near your property allows you to furnish it, remodel it, show it to applicants, host house activities, and manage move-ins and move-outs. Someone needs to perform these duties, and if you are physically available, you won't have to pay someone else to do them. Additionally, performing this work enables you to learn the ins and outs of co-living on the job. This is precisely how I developed most of the systems in this book. I encountered issues with the properties in my local market, visited the property to fix the problem, and documented the solution. This can be done remotely, but I learned from my mistakes faster attending to them personally as I was within a ten-minute drive of most of my properties.

Lastly, purchasing in your local market allows you to develop in-person relationships with your agents, lenders, contractors, cleaners, and handyperson. Meeting members of your team in person allows you to read each other better and determine if each will fit the other's business well. While you can build your team remotely, nothing beats good, old-fashioned, face-to-face interactions.

There are significant benefits of purchasing locally, but if you want to scale your portfolio, the goal should be to build relationships and systems that eventually allow you to remove yourself from the process.

Investing Remotely

If you analyze your local market and find it unsuitable for the co-living strategy, you must invest remotely. We'll discuss how to perform this analysis shortly, in the market analysis section. Managing many strangers in a single house from hundreds of miles away may sound daunting, but co-living is well suited to be run from afar. In Part IV: Managing a Co-Living Property, we dive into the specifics of co-living management. But for now, know that there are many tasks that can be performed by your existing residents and other team members: having your residents perform property tours for you, having your cleaners do the move-out inspections, enlisting your handyman to perform check-ins, and more. To be successful from afar, you'll be highly reliant on these team members, as well as your real estate agent and potentially a property manager.

Investing remotely forces you to spend money rather than time on the property setup, cleanings, remodeling, and maintenance. Depending on your situation, this may be a good or bad idea. If you can support this cost, it will do wonders for your business, as it frees you up to focus on more critical business tasks, making it possible to scale your portfolio to new heights.

Additionally, investing remotely opens up your investment opportunities and enables you to select the best market possible. Considering the number of cities in the U.S., the odds that your backyard has the best metrics for co-living are very low. You may find better returns elsewhere if you are willing to expand your horizons.

Be wary, however, of being skewed by the enticing returns a remote market may show. An essential piece of data that is hard to quantify is your unfair advantage in your local market. Perhaps your brother-in-law is an investor and real estate agent who will work extra hard to find you the best deal. Maybe you own a construction company and can remodel for 50 percent of the cost that you'd pay in a remote market. Consider these factors when investing locally or remotely; they could be beneficial enough to support investing locally, even if the data may indicate that a remote market has higher returns.

Market Analysis

Market analysis is the process of sifting through many cities to find the top handful that are the best for you. Even if you think that investing locally is the approach you'd like to take, market analysis is still an important step if you want to be a great investor, as it can confirm or refute your gut feeling about your market.

Many investors take a less-informed approach, entering a market because of a top ten list they read or a friend told them about it. These are fine factors to consider, but if you are going to invest hundreds of thousands of dollars over time, a better approach is to broaden your horizons and take full control of the analysis.

Your Goals and Metrics of Importance

The first step of market analysis has nothing to do with numbers. Just ask yourself: What are my goals? With the thousands of markets in the United States, none are the best *for you* until you know what you want. Some may be great for appreciation, some for cash flow, and some may have a lower-cost barrier to entry.

I encourage you to spend ten minutes brainstorming what your ideal market looks like and what it provides you. Scribble any phrase or word that comes to mind. Ask questions like:

- Do I want cash flow or appreciation most?
- What is my property budget?
- Does my ideal market reside in a particular geographic area?
- Is there a certain demographic of renter I want to provide housing to?

Once you have answered these questions, think about the types of data that can be used to locate this market. Don't worry about where or how you'll find this data. Instead, just write down any metrics that would describe your ideal market. Here are some examples:

- High population growth - indicates strong appreciation and rent growth
- High historical appreciation - indicates strong future appreciation
- High historical rent growth - indicates strong future rent growth
- High studio apartment unaffordability - indicates need for cheaper housing
- High room rents - indicates strong cash flow
- Number of rooms listed for rent - indicates room supply
- People interested in rooms for rent - indicates room demand
- Purchase price - indicates affordability for investors with limited funds
- Renter demographics - describes the type of residents in your pool of renters

Remember that these indicators are not guarantees. For example, just because a market has seen outsized appreciation over the last five years does not mean that trend will continue. However, it may show that that market has the fundamentals that can lead to more appreciation in the future.

Now that you have a list of metrics useful in your analysis, spend some time trying to find data for each. I'll provide some starting points for the example metrics I presented.

Phase One: Surface-Level Research

Analyzing markets to find the one that is right for you involves many steps, but performing them in a well thought-out order will ease the workload. For example, you don't want to start by researching the co-living laws for one hundred cities when you can't afford to purchase in most of them anyway.

I recommend storing this market data in a spreadsheet (Microsoft Excel or Google Sheets); however, if you are unfamiliar with digital spreadsheets, you can use a pen and paper.

First, determine which of your criteria is most limiting; this will help you create a pretty small list of initial markets instead of starting with all 19,000 markets in the United States. For example, if one of your criteria is that the city must have 500,000 people, that will give you a starting list of only thirty-eight markets. If you want to target military members, your starting list could be limited to markets with military bases, which would filter you down to 150 markets.

Once you have this moderately sized list of markets, you can gather additional information regarding metrics you deemed important. From there, you'll filter down to three to ten markets that most align with your goals.

This approach is great, but if you are a data nut like me and like diving into spreadsheets, then you can check out this guide to how I performed research to filter all 19,000 cities down to a short list for myself: www.BiggerPockets.com/CoLivingBonus.

Now, let's discuss some of the data I consider most important and where to find them.

POPULATION

Population is the number of people that live in a market, while population growth measures the increase or decrease in the number of people in a market. A positive population growth means more people are moving to than moving from a market, and a negative population growth means more people are leaving than coming to a market.

When you compare markets, those with higher positive growth are more likely to experience increasing property values and rents in the future. This is due to increased demand, caused by the influx of residents, which strains the existing supply.

The most accurate source for population data is the United States Census Bureau. The actual population census is taken every ten years; however, the bureau also estimates the populations for each city annually, providing more up-to-date information. Their website can be challenging to navigate, but you'll likely want to search for their "City and Town Population Totals" table.

You may want to filter out markets below a specific population. Although it is possible to use the co-living strategy in smaller markets, the larger a market is, the more residents there are to choose from. Additionally, the larger a market is, the more contractors, cleaners, and repair professionals available to you.

The population over time is even more telling. Knowing that one city has one million people and another has 600,000 today doesn't tell you the population trend, which is arguably more important. The million-person city can be a bad contender if it had 1,100,000 people the previous year. This would mean everyone is moving out of town! So, you want to determine the direction of population growth.

First, you must establish a time range over which to calculate the growth. Population growth should be used as an indicator of long-term market health. Over two years, a healthy market could see a slight decline, but it could have high population growth over a longer time span. A simple and effective approach is to look at the table you gathered from the U.S. Census Bureau and grab today's population and the population from ten, fifteen, or twenty years ago for the cities of interest, then divide today's population by the past population. The higher the resulting number, the more the population has multiplied. A more complex but equally effective approach is using the RRI function in Microsoft Excel or Google Sheets to determine the annual population increase. This function helps you calculate the annualized growth rate, which is the compounded change in a quantity over time.

For example, if a property increased from $200,000 to $400,000 over ten years, you'd know it doubled. More important, though, is the annualized growth rate, which tells you it compounded at about 7.2 percent per year. The same principle applies to population growth. RRI tells you how fast a city grows, not just the before and after numbers.

HISTORICAL APPRECIATION AND RENT GROWTH

Historical appreciation measures property values over time. Just because a market has experienced increasing property values in the past doesn't mean that it will continue to in the future, but it does mean that strong market fundamentals may still exist: lots of jobs, natural attractions (mountains, oceans), low income taxes, or constrained housing geography. This is more of a lagging indicator but can still help tell a market's story.

Historical rent growth measures the increase or decrease in rent over time. This data can provide information on a market's past that may help inform its future. A history of increasing rents means there has been more demand than supply, and if enough supply isn't produced, this trend can continue.

To calculate historical appreciation and rent growth, you need to determine a period over which to gather data and retrieve the values to compare the beginning and end. A longer time frame will inform an average that is more likely to hold in the future.

Zillow is an excellent resource for property value and rent data. Their housing data page gives you access to data at the state, county, city, zip code, and neighborhood levels over time. You can download the city dataset, select your start and end dates, and divide the end value by the start value. Alternatively, you can again use the RRI function to calculate the annual growth.

Depending on your circumstances, you may also want to filter out markets that exceed a specific property value. Coming out of college, my wife and I had a limited amount of capital to contribute to the down payment of our first house hack. When we were selecting a market, we excluded cities like Denver because we simply couldn't afford to purchase there. Instead, we focused on markets we could afford.

ROOM RENTS

Determining standard room rent is crucial when selecting a market for co-living. Knowing the average room rents will be helpful not only in choosing a market but also in analyzing specific properties and eventually listing the rooms for rent. There isn't a database centralizing the room rents for various markets, so you'll have to find this information yourself.

You are still a few steps away from purchasing a property, so you don't need to know exactly what room rents are. You just need a decent understanding of them to help you filter down to the handful of markets you want to investigate further.

One great resource for estimating room rent is the Room Rent Calculator I built at www.BiggerPockets.com/CoLivingBonus. This tool provides rent estimates for various markets nationwide, factoring in variables like furnishing type, bathroom type, and room size.

Alternatively, you can estimate the rate yourself. A standard room that shares a bathroom, including all utilities, will rent for around 1 percent of the typical salary in the area.

For example, if a city has a median salary of $70,000, a room will likely be rented for $700/month. This number isn't pulled out of thin air; it is based on some simple math. I've found that room rentals are in demand among the bottom 35 percent of earners, as studio apartments are their cheapest alternative yet too expensive. The median salary multiplied by 35 percent yields the income that this resident makes. Additionally, for residents to live comfortably, an industry rule says they should spend 30 percent of their salary on housing. Lastly, the salary needs to be converted to a monthly figure.

$$\text{Room Rent Estimate} = \text{Annual Salary} \; \frac{35\% \times 30\%}{12} \approx \text{Annual Salary} \times 1\%$$

For this estimate, you only need to know a market's typical salary to estimate the room rent. The best salary resource I've found is PayScale. If you search for "PayScale salary in <city>," you'll find the information.

RENTAL UNAFFORDABILITY

Rental unaffordability is the percentage of a renter's income spent on rent, which essentially describes how difficult it is for someone of a certain income to afford a particular rental. This becomes most useful when calculating the unaffordability of a studio apartment because your target resident is most likely considering this option since it is one of the cheapest. If studios are expensive relative to income, that indicates residents would benefit from a more affordable housing product like a room.

You have already found the typical salary for the markets of interest. Now you need to find the studio rents. Apartments.com is an excellent resource for this data. If you search "Apartments.com <city> average studio rent," you'll find this information. When calculating unaffordability, a higher result means that studios are more unaffordable, and thus, a room may be a cheaper alternative.

$$\text{Studio Unaffordability} = \frac{\text{Monthly Studio Rent} \times 12}{\text{Average Annual Income}}$$

You may also use this data to calculate how much a resident could save if they were renting a room instead of a studio apartment. The calculation below will give you the discount the resident can receive by renting your space.

$$\text{Studio to Room Discount} = 1 - \frac{\text{Room Rent}}{\text{Studio Rent}}$$

ROOM RENT-TO-PRICE RATIO

The 1 percent rule states that if a property's monthly rent divided by its purchase price is 1 percent or greater, it may be an excellent rental property. This is simply a rent-to-price ratio. Essentially, it tells you the bang for your buck a property can give you. For every dollar a property costs, you'll get a certain number of dollars in return every year. It is a handy metric to help you infer which markets may have the highest returns. In this case, you'll want to use the room rent instead of the total rent that the 1 percent rule uses.

You'll see that room rent-to-price ratios don't come close to 1 percent. This is because you are only accounting for the rent of a single room rather than the rent for the whole property. In reality, you'll rent many bedrooms, but just leave that out of this equation for now. Instead, you'll focus on finding the markets where single rooms rent for a high amount while the properties cost a low amount. During the property analysis stage, which will be discussed in Chapter 6: Selecting a Property, you'll factor in the number of rooms on a property-by-property basis.

You already have the data for this calculation. Previously, you estimated the room rental rates. You also found the property value when calculating historical appreciation, which is a good substitute for the purchase price.

$$\text{Room Rent-to-Price Ratio} = \frac{\text{Monthly Room Rent}}{\text{Average Property Purchase Price}}$$

DEMOGRAPHICS

When sifting through markets, it is crucial to identify your target resident. There are a variety of residents looking to rent a room. Identifying which you want to serve will help narrow down the market you invest in.

While you can select a market and property that caters to a particular resident type, once you are operating and seeking applicants, you cannot target a specific demographic. Instead, you must market fairly to all, approving applicants who pass your screening criteria and agree with the Fair Housing Act and other state laws.

Low-Income Workers

If you've ever researched mid-term rentals, you know that traveling nurses are the primary tenant type that investors seek. Low-income workers are like the traveling nurses of the co-living space. They are a reliable resident type that can be found in many markets and can make up a large portion of your residents. In fact, low-income workers make up close to 50 percent of the residents in my properties.

To broadly define this group, these people make less than the average wage and need to rent a room to remain financially healthy as the alternatives are too expensive for them. My portfolio includes minimum-wage workers, security guards, social workers, schoolteachers, warehouse workers, and more. Some investors may question the viability of renting to low-income workers, but I have found many great residents in this group. They are great people who just happen to make less money than the rest of the market. With the excellent screening practices I'll present in Chapter 11: Finding Residents, you can find the low earners who will treat your property and the other residents with respect.

The minimum wage worker cannot afford to rent their own apartment unless they have a cosigner, so they've probably been searching for affordable housing without success. A well-managed room rental is a welcome relief when they find it because they can qualify for it themselves without spending most of their income. Also, you can feel good about serving this group. While the government is searching for a solution to the affordable housing crisis, you can sleep soundly knowing that you've found a solution and are implementing it, helping many in your community.

A downside to renting to this group is that they occasionally have issues paying rent. This is less of a problem than you'd think, because your room likely costs around 30 percent of their income, but it is more of a risk than with other groups in this list. The justifications are often reasonable, like getting sick and missing a week of work, so you must consider how to respond to these situations. I provide a week's grace period on rent payments, and this is typically enough time for them to get caught up.

To determine whether a market supports this group, just look at the studio unaffordability you calculated previously. You could also look up poverty levels for your markets of interest.

College Students

College students are one of the more obvious demographics when considering room rentals. Students are accustomed to living in dorms, so a room rental provides a similar experience for a lower price. Also, it is usually an upgrade because they don't have roommates anymore; they have housemates.

One benefit of renting to students is that they almost always have a parent cosigning. This is helpful in two ways. First, the parent, who probably makes a good salary, is often overqualified to pay for a cheap room, meaning you are unlikely to have collection issues. Second, you will have the parent's contact information, so you can rely on the parent for backup if you have problems with the student. Also, students will usually want to live with their friends, so if you capture one student, you could capture many of their friends, making finding residents much easier.

Some downsides are that, depending on the student, they may put more wear and tear on the property. Younger residents tend to be less mature and less respectful of the premises. Additionally, students often search for leases that last for the fall and spring semesters and may want to vacate for the summer months. So, you could experience vacancies in the summer but steady occupancy during the academic year.

If this is your target resident, you'll likely want to gather data on university enrollment nationwide. Generating a list of cities with large enrollment is a great starting place, as the more students that are enrolled in college, the more residents you'll have to choose from.

Military Members

Military members are my bread and butter as they make up about 50 percent of my residents.

Lower-rank members are ideal co-living residents. First, they are experienced with shared housing, likely coming straight from the barracks and looking for off-base housing. Second, they are usually single, so they aren't looking for a large, lavish place to live. Third, they don't have a lot of possessions and thus have minimal storage needs. Fourth, military members have been conditioned to be respectful and clean, causing few issues with other housemates. Lastly, they receive a housing stipend that is often much higher than room rent, so they pay rent and get to pocket the excess stipend—a win-win!

As for downsides, I can have a high concentration of move-out notices during the permanent change of station (PCS) season. This is when members receive their orders to change locations. This usually means members are also moving to my market, but it still leads to a higher workload: processing paperwork, scheduling move-outs, etc. Also, military members cannot abide by a lease's end date when they receive orders, so you could move someone in only to have them move out a month or two later if they receive new orders.

The military releases a demographics profile on an annual basis that details the number of members stationed at each base. If you want to rent to military members, this can provide data to help start your market selection.

Young Professionals and Interns

Young professionals are recent college graduates. Room rentals are an easy transition for them, as they were recently in college, living with housemates or in dorms. They comprise a smaller portion of my portfolio, but I rent to some, primarily young engineers looking to build their savings. Many other professions also fit this description.

The most significant benefit to serving this group is that they often have overqualified income for your rental, so the probability of them missing a rental payment is very low.

Their income level is also a downside because many become subject to lifestyle creep. Once their lease is up, I've found that many of them decide to move into a place by themselves since they can afford it.

College interns are found in the same markets as young professionals because the same companies hire them. The difference is that interns have lower incomes and need room rentals more than young professionals. Unfortunately, they often spend a short time at the internship before returning to school, although there are exceptions. The amount of time varies based on the employer. The recruitment departments of the companies in your markets of interest can tell you whether interns are seasonal in that market. If interns are only there in the summer, they can only help you fill short vacancies in that season. If they are there year-round, they could become one of your primary resident types.

Cities that are suited for these groups are the ones with the lowest median age and highest number of college graduates. On city-data.com, you can find both of these data points. To research further, you can look for cities with high concentrations of finance, technology, and health industries, as many college graduates and interns work in these fields.

Traveling Workers

Traveling workers can include health care professionals, construction managers and workers, pilots and flight attendants, and others.

This group of traveling workers can be served by "crash pads." Crash pads are properties targeted at mobile professionals seeking affordable housing options outside of their primary residence and near their primary work location. Crash pads often provide multiple beds in each room. These workers are away so often that the number of people in a room on a given night is minimal, although it is rented to many. This subgroup is a stable group of residents, as they can afford room rentals and are unlikely to leave your property in favor of another since they spend much of their time traveling and do not need much space.

The rest of the traveling workers are seeking flexible and cheap housing at their temporary destination and have a high turnover rate. They typically search for month-to-month leases, as their contracts can be extended. Be prepared for short stays, although extensions could work in your favor.

To find markets that support renting to pilots and flight attendants, filter to markets with airport hubs. Each airline will have specific airport hubs where it operates heavily. The flight attendants and pilots the company hires mostly have their primary residences around these hubs. To find markets that support other traveling workers, filter to markets with lots of ongoing construction and high demand for medical services.

NARROWING IT DOWN

At this point, you have a lot of data about many cities. Let's narrow it down to three to ten markets you may want to pursue. Making a hard cut and selecting your favorites will help you move forward with less analysis paralysis.

If you know which markets you prefer by glancing through your list, then great! You can move on to phase two with this short list. If you still have many markets on your list, here's a mathematical approach you can use to narrow it down.

As a simple example, let's say you have the list of markets seen in Table 1, and for each market, you care most about studio unaffordability and population growth.

Market	Studio Unaffordability	Population Growth
Market A	30%	5%
Market B	40%	3%
Market C	50%	4%

Table 1. Studio unaffordability and population growth

The higher the studio's unaffordability, the better, as it indicates that people need cheaper housing. The higher the population growth, the better, because there may be higher appreciation and rental demand in the future.

If you were to sort these markets based on studio unaffordability, you'd see that Market C is best, followed by B and A. If you were to sort based on population growth, you'd see that Market A is best, followed by C and B. So, how do you combine the information and determine the best overall market? There is a mathematical approach you can take called weighted scoring.

Weighted scoring involves assigning each metric a weight that describes how important that data is to you. Then, you can use some math to calculate a score that shows how well that market fits your personal preferences.

First, you'll calculate scores without weighting. All you are doing here is determining, for each market and data type, who the winners and losers are. To do this, divide the data for each market by the highest value in the dataset. In the example, for population growth, 5 percent is the highest, so you'll divide each data point by 5 percent: 5 percent/5 percent, 3 percent/5 percent, and 4 percent/5 percent. You can see in Table 2 that market A scores 100 percent, which is the highest on the list, so it is the best. Market B scores 60 percent, the lowest in the list, so it is the worst. For studio unaffordability, if you followed the same process, you'd see that market C scores 100 percent while market A scores 60 percent.

Market	Studio Unaffordability (Score)	Population Growth (Score)
A	60%	100%
B	80%	60%
C	100%	80%

Table 2. Studio unaffordability and population growth scores

Lastly, you'll apply weights to the scores to emphasize the metrics you care most about and combine them to give a final score. Think about each metric in your table and how much you care about each. For this example, you might care most about rental demand, so you give studio unaffordability a weight of 70 percent while giving population growth a weight of 30 percent. Maybe you care more about future appreciation, so you set the population growth weight to 60 percent and studio unaffordability weight to 40 percent. This is totally up to you and your investing goals; just ensure that all the weights add up to 100 percent. For this example, I'll use 70 percent for studio unaffordability and 30 percent for population growth.

Multiply each score by its corresponding weight. Then add up those weighted scores for each market. This is the total weighted score. You can see the final example results in Table 3.

Market	Studio Unaffordability (Weighted Score: 70%)	Population Growth (Weighted Score: 30%)	Total Weighted Score
A	42%	30%	72%
B	56%	18%	74%
C	70%	24%	94%

Table 3. Total, studio unaffordability, and population weighted scores

That was a lot of work, but now you know which markets are best based on your investing preferences. In the example, market C scored the best, with a total weighted score of 94 percent, followed by B and A. The order would have been different if population growth had been favored more than studio unaffordability. This is why there is no best market for co-living, short-term rentals, or any other strategy. You can determine which markets are best *for you* using this weighted scoring method.

Once your entire dataset has been scored, you can select the top three to ten markets for your short list and proceed with phase two.

Phase Two: Deep Research

In the first phase of the research, you gathered easy-to-find data and made some calculations that could point you toward markets best suited for co-living. In this phase, you will further scrutinize your short list by confirming some of your approximations and gathering qualitative data.

OCCUPANCY LAWS

You should understand the legality of co-living before entering a market. This involves researching the views of any governing body on co-living, such as the city, county, and state.

The restriction you'll see most often is the number of people allowed to live in a house. Such regulations usually occur at the city level. The law is typically written as several unrelated persons allowed in a unit. For example, "Up to four persons unrelated to each other by blood, marriage, or legal adoption, living together as a single housekeeping unit." Be sure to check for county and state regulations too, although they are less common.

You can search online to find out if regulations exist and what they are; however, the information is difficult to find. Instead, I'd recommend contacting the city's planning or zoning office. By searching the web for "<city> Planning Office" or "<city> Zoning Office," you'll likely find their web pages. Ideally, you'll see their email on this page. If not, you may find a contact form to fill out. I'd caution against calling them, as their response will be undocumented. It is best to have their response written so that you have a record in case there is ever an issue. In your written request, explain that you want to provide high-quality housing to your target resident, and ask if there are any restrictions against having a certain number of unrelated people in a single-family house.

If you'll be subject to restrictive occupancy laws based on the number of residents you plan to have, keep digging.

Occupancy laws are in flux across the country. Co-living is becoming increasingly accepted as a solution to housing affordability, with some states fully legalizing it. As of the writing of this book (2024), three states have implemented policies that remove occupancy limits for many property types state wide and prevent local governments from setting limits. In 2021, Washington and Oregon enacted such policies, followed by Colorado in 2024. I'd expect more and more states to adopt such policies, assuming renter affordability remains a hardship.

While some states are reevaluating occupancy limits, many cities are doing the same. In your research, you'll probably read some ordinances that read "A group of not more than five persons, excluding servants." Servants? These laws are ripe for reevaluation. With an online search, you could find what bills are being voted on in the state right now, and you may be able to judge the sentiment and predict which way the decision will go.

Talking to locals and searching forums to see if the occupancy laws are enforced can be helpful. For example, while co-living is totally legal across Colorado now, it wasn't always that way. Previously, my city had a "no more than five unrelated persons" law. Research showed that the ordinance was created in the 1970s. In 2019, short-term rental regulations set the occupancy limits to two people per bedroom or fewer. So, although this didn't apply to my longer-term rentals, it gave me an indication of how the city was thinking more recently. Additionally, from talking with real estate agents and other investors in the area, no one had heard of any enforcement preventing more than five unrelated persons.

When deciding to enter a market, weigh all of this information, along with your own risk tolerance.

If the risk is too high to operate a single-family house using the co-living strategy, and you are still interested in the market, see if you can get creative! Finding a solution in a market that others dismiss because of the regulations can make you one of the few operators in town. Some cities will have boarding house or rooming house zonings, allowing many unrelated people to live there. In this case, you may purchase a property already zoned this way, or you may be able to buy a property and get it rezoned. This could be costly, but it could be worth it if it makes you the only game in town. Don't be scared of hard work!

EMPLOYERS

A strong market will have strong sources of employment for your residents. This is less of a number in the spreadsheet and more of a fact about the area. When looking into new markets, search the web for the largest employers in the city. You want to see employers that have and will stand the test of time rather than some oil company rumored to go out of business or some factory scheduled to be shut down. It is helpful to know if these businesses are growing because growing businesses hire more employees. Some of these new employees will come from out of the city, driving up the demand for rental properties, lowering your vacancy, and increasing your rent. By searching the web for each of these businesses, you'll probably find articles talking about the stability of these businesses and whether they have significant growth plans.

To take it a step further, you can look into the workers' salaries at each company. If you search Indeed for the company, you'll find the average salary for many positions. For example, my local hospital has most jobs paying $50,000/year or less, which would require more than 30 percent of their income to go to a studio apartment, meaning they need co-living housing.

ROOM RENTAL DEMAND TEST

Confirming that the residents of the city you are researching want rooms for rent is a crucial step in the process. While all the data you've collected so far can point to markets that may be great for co-living, this is a critical piece of the puzzle and needs to be confirmed.

While you could look at room rental listing services and see what is currently available, this only describes the supply and not the demand. There could be 1,000 rooms for rent in a city, but if there are only ten people per year looking for a room to rent, then it is not a good market for co-living.

I came very close to pulling the trigger on a new market that I assumed was great for co-living. I had selected an agent, they had toured the property, and I had calculated the offer I planned to submit. As it would have been my first out-of-state market, I felt some fear before submitting the offer and decided to post a Facebook Marketplace advertisement for a room in that market, hoping to see a lot of interest. Over seven days, only one person messaged me. I would have been in deep water had I purchased it. Now, it is a required part of my market research to post a room ad, so I know that people in the market want this product.

You may feel like this is a slimy business tactic: posting an ad for a room you don't own. Such ad testing is standard in many areas of business. In Tim Ferriss's *4-Hour Workweek*, he talks about the concept of micro-testing. "Micro-testing involves using inexpensive advertisements to test consumer response to a product before manufacturing."[6] Ferriss uses examples of creating ads for products that have not been created to see if there is enough consumer demand to warrant its production. That is precisely the idea behind the room rental demand test: to see if this is a product that the market wants.

The goal of this test is to collect information by counting the number of people who are interested in a room.

Creating the Advertisement

The first step is to create the advertisement. I'll dive deeper into the listing services where you can post your rooms in Chapter 11: Finding Residents, but I'd recommend posting this test on Facebook Marketplace and Roomies for now. Facebook Marketplace and Roomies make up a large portion of my inquiries, so posting on these will provide adequate results without listing on all other platforms. You could add other platforms into the mix, but be aware that many have measures and verifications that prevent you from posting an ad for a property you don't own.

---

6   Tim Ferris, *The 4-Hour Workweek* (Harmony Books, 2009).

When creating the ad, you'll need to select a location. Start by looking at neighborhoods near the places your target renter will visit frequently: work, college, downtown, etc. If those neighborhoods have purchase prices significantly higher than the market average, you may want to remove them from the list, as this will result in lower cash flow than expected.

Once you find a neighborhood you think will draw some attention, "walk" around on Google Street View and find a property with good curb appeal and decent parking. To be cautious, search the address on Zillow and ensure it isn't currently for sale. Listing a room for rent in a property that is for sale may throw some red flags. If it isn't for sale, then proceed!

You don't need to have actual pictures of the inside of the house. Instead, just use some boilerplate pictures of a furnished kitchen, a furnished living room, a furnished bathroom, and an unfurnished room. Most of the rooms in the property you buy will end up sharing a bathroom; that is the type of room to list—not a room with a private bathroom.

Room pricing can be tricky, but starting with the estimate you previously calculated based on the market's median salary is an excellent place to start. You can also take this time to look at the room comparables in the area and adjust your starting rent if needed.

The rental description at this stage can be simple. For now, you can mention that a housekeeper cleans the shared areas regularly, shared supplies like toilet paper are provided, and the kitchen and living room are fully furnished. You can also describe how close the property is to employment and entertainment centers if you'd like.

Collecting the Data

Now that the ad is posted, you need a data collection method. You could tally the number of people who send you a message, but it is tough to know how many of those are seriously interested or would be able to qualify. Instead, I'd recommend creating a Google Form asking some basic questions about their credit history and income. Make one for each market you post in to keep the data separate. Here is an example Google Form that you can copy and use: www.BiggerPockets.com/CoLivingBonus.

You'll get lots of "Is this available?" messages. I'll talk more later about how best to respond to interested renters in Chapter 11: Finding

Residents, but at this research stage, it is best to reply to everyone with "Yes, that room is available! Please fill out this quick form, and then we'll get back to you: <form link>." Remember, the goal here is just to collect data. If some people are turned off by this message, that is okay. Most folks serious about signing a lease will take thirty seconds to click the link and answer some questions.

Reviewing the Data

Give the ad some time to gain interest—at least one week, but the longer the better. Then, review the Google Form to see how many people have filled it out.

Do you have enough inquiries to say this market supports co-living? Well, it will depend on a few factors.

- How many bedrooms do you plan to have?
- How quickly do you want to fully occupy the property?
- How many days was the ad listed for?
- You were only listed on some platforms, so how much greater would the number of forms be if you were listed on all platforms?
- What portion of people who filled out the form would sign a lease?

By this point, you know I have a science brain and rely on math and data to make investing decisions. The equation below may look complex, but it will help you determine how many interest forms you need to give a market a thumbs-up or -down. I won't oversimplify by saying, "Make sure you get at least five interest forms, and you're good!" because this is a crucial step that depends on multiple factors.

This equation helps account for those variables and gives you a data-driven benchmark.

$$\text{Interest Forms Needed} = \frac{\text{Bedrooms in House}}{\text{Desired Weeks to Fully Occupy}} \times \frac{\text{Days Ad Listed}}{7} \times \frac{\text{Partial Listing Scaling Factor}}{\text{Lease Conversion Rate}}$$

As an example, I usually buy eight-bedroom properties and aim to fill them within eight weeks. Let's assume that I had this test ad listed for ten days. Based on the data in my business, Facebook Marketplace and Roomies bring in around 45 percent of the interest forms, while other listing services make up the remainder. Lastly, in my experience, 10 percent of the interest forms convert to a signed lease, although this could be different for your business.

$$\frac{8 \text{ Bedrooms}}{8 \text{ Weeks}} \times \frac{10 \text{ days}}{7} \times \frac{0.45}{0.1} = 6.42 \text{ Forms}$$

In this example, I need to see at least 6.42 interest forms completed over the ten-day period to meet my target of filling an eight-bedroom house within eight weeks.

If you find that the number of forms you received exceeds your threshold, that is excellent! If you did not receive enough interest forms, then it could be:

- The room rent is too high.
- The specific location doesn't have sufficient demand for room rentals.
- The market, as a whole, does not have enough demand for room rentals.

Start by assuming the rent is too high and lower the price by $50–$100, then run the test for another week. In theory, if you dropped the price enough, I'm sure you'd get enough interest, but deals may not be profitable at that rent. So, consider that and decide when to give up and move on.

If you still don't see enough interest, assume that the neighborhood doesn't support room rentals and move the listing to another neighborhood. If you used the form I previously provided, you'll see a question asking which parts of town the interested party most wants to live in. Diving deeper into these areas of town as your next target could be a good idea.

Continue adjusting rent and moving the listing as many times as necessary. At some point, you may realize that this market isn't ideal for co-living, and you can strike it off your list.

Talk to Locals

The last step of phase two is to talk with those who live and operate in the area. This step is often overlooked by anyone looking to invest in a remote market, but it is the most valuable.

While you were crunching numbers in your spreadsheet about population growth and looking up the major employers, local investors and service providers spent their time in that market, observing those trends and getting the inside scoop. That doesn't mean your research was a waste of time; it just means that there is another side to the story you have yet to uncover.

Finding a local investor experienced in co-living may prove difficult. Still, investors using other strategies can give you insights into the general trends of the market: job growth, population growth, areas to buy in, places to avoid, occupancy law enforcement, demographics, and more. Simply asking for a ten-minute phone call or in-person meeting if you live close enough will reveal so much.

There are many ways to find these investors. First, you can search the BiggerPockets forums for posts about this city. In the comments, you can identify profiles of the folks that operate there and message them. You can also search local Facebook groups.

While you are at it, ask them which real estate agents, lenders, and contractors they prefer. Having those recommendations on hand will be important if you decide to enter this market.

In Chapter 6: Selecting a Property, we'll dive deep into how to find the best real estate agent, and in Chapter 9: Management Strategy, we'll discuss finding property managers. For now, though, consider chatting with a few of these professionals to gain further insights. As many agents and property managers are not co-living experts, they may steer you to neighborhoods that are best for families or traditional long-term rental investments, which may not be best for co-living. So, rather than relying on them to provide specifics about the areas of town, rely on them for high-level market information such as migration, upcoming developments, and property tax or insurance concerns. Also, remember that they want your business at the end of the day and are highly incentivized to feed you sugary information, so trust but verify any information they give you.

Phase Three: Confirm Your Research

You started with a list of tens, hundreds, or thousands of markets to invest in; now, you've reduced it to two or three that best fit your investing goals and style. Congratulations! The very last step is to confirm your research. This involves diving into real property listings and laying your virtual eyes on the city.

First, hop on Zillow or an alternative listing site. Click through the pictures and see what insights you can glean. The idea here is to get a feel for the houses in the city. Are all of the interiors outdated? If so, do you have the skills, and are you willing to put in the work yourself or hire the workers to remodel them? Are the neighborhoods comfortable for the average working class tenant to live in? Are most of the listings small, 1,200-square-foot, two-bedroom, one-bath houses, or are they large, 2,500-square-foot, four-bedroom, three-bath houses?

I know this "feel good" approach is much different from the mathematical approach you've taken, but you've already determined that the numbers look suitable for these top markets. Now, it is essential that you like the market you select and that you can see yourself owning a co-living property here.

In my market research, some cities have survived to phase three, but then I found the whole town was filled with hundred-year-old homes that I had no interest in or skills to remodel. Some investors out there with great contractors and a skill set for managing them will make a killing in that market, but I know that isn't for me. Some cities I've looked at just have tiny houses, 1,500 square feet or less on average. Some investors will have the skills to build an accessory dwelling unit in the backyard and have incredible cash flow, but I'm not interested in that.

Don't be afraid to filter out a market at this stage; you must be excited about the market you decide to enter. If you filter out all of your top contenders, return to the Narrowing It Down section of phase one, select the next three to ten markets that appear to be good performers, and go through phases two and three again.

Once you've filtered down to one or two markets in which you are excited to own property, you've finished phase three!

Chapter 4

Preparing to Enter a Market

Now that you've completed the lengthy (but critical) market analysis, it is time to put the last few pieces of the puzzle together before you purchase your first co-living property. When you enter a new market, you'll need a real estate agent, a lender, and an insurance agent. You may also want a co-living property manager on your team; however, they are not required for the acquisition process, so we'll chat more about property managers in Chapter 9: Management Strategy.

Finding the Best Real Estate Agent

Your real estate agent is the most important member of your team. They are your ticket into the real estate world, as they will most likely have referrals for the best lenders, insurance brokers, and contractors.

Similar to selecting the best market, to find the best real estate agent, you will generate an extensive list of agents to filter through until you are left with a small list to choose from. Don't worry—this is much easier and quicker than choosing a market. There have been many chapters in books about finding great agents. *Long-Distance Real Estate Investing* by David Greene (www.BiggerPockets.com/ReadLongDistance) is one of the best, so feel free to reference that for a very comprehensive method. Here, I'll just provide a quick list of places you should pull from when generating your list.

- BiggerPockets Agent Finder (www.BiggerPockets.com/BookAgent)
- BiggerPockets Forums posts (www.BiggerPockets.com/BookForums)
- Make your own BiggerPockets Forums post
- Local Facebook group posts
- Make your own local Facebook group post
- Ask the local investors you found during market research
- Search YouTube for "Real Estate Investing <city>" and reach out to the host of that channel
- Search Meetup.com for real estate meetups and attend (if local) or message the hosts (if remote)

Now that you have this list, text/email all of them with a message like:

> Hey <name>! I'm looking for an agent to help me buy large properties (2,500+ square feet with 5+ bedrooms) that I will rent out by the room. I'm looking to buy three this year and even more next year. You've come highly recommended, and I'd love to schedule a phone call to chat more with you. Are you free today or tomorrow?

You are looking to learn a few things when you send that message. First, do they reply? Most agents on your list probably won't answer. Second, how quickly do they respond? You want someone who will always get back to you within a couple of hours. If it takes someone a day or longer to reach back out, they are either too disorganized or too busy to give you the required attention. Third, are they interested at all? Some agents aren't interested in working with investors.

Now that you've scheduled some calls, prepare for what to say. Think of this call as an interview and treat it like one. Grill the agent on any topics you think are essential and weed out anyone who may be inadequate and inexperienced. I'd recommend asking:

- How long have you lived in this market?
- How long have you worked as an agent in this market?
- What do you like about this market?
- What do you not like about this market?
- How many properties have you closed in the past twelve months?
- Do you have any investment properties?
- If so, how did you find these properties, and what kind of returns do you receive?
- Do you have experience working as an investor agent?
- What type of support team members do you have great contacts for? I'm thinking of lenders, insurance agents, contractors, handymen, cleaners, etc.
- What does your team look like? Do agents work under you or alongside you? Is there someone to handle the paperwork? Are you doing most of it yourself?

Of these questions, the most important is if they invest themselves and work with investors. I know of many investors who tried to work with their mom's best friend, who happened to be an agent, and didn't receive the service an investor needs. I have used an agent who worked with investors but didn't invest themselves. While this worked decently, now that I've worked with an agent who is also an investor, I will never go back. Being able to walk through a house and bounce remodel ideas and budget estimates off each other has been a game changer.

The next-most important question is what sort of contacts they have. An agent with these connections will save you hours of work. Since these team members would be referrals, they'd likely be of higher quality than the ones you'd find on your own.

After writing down all the answers to these questions, consider the demeanor and attitude of the agent. Does this seem like someone you'd enjoy talking to daily while building your business?

With all of this information in mind, make a selection. While you can choose multiple agents to work with, I wouldn't recommend it. Having a single, highly competent agent you are committed to working with will ensure the best deals get brought to you, as they aren't wondering if they'll get the commission. This doesn't mean you can't continue conversations with other agents and ask them for listings that meet your criteria, but most of your focus should be spent with a single agent you develop a rewarding relationship with.

Lending

Before you start looking at specific properties, you'll need to identify a lender and determine the type of loan you will use, as it may have some influence on the property you choose. If you chose a rock star real estate agent, they will have a few lenders you can interview and choose from of similar caliber.

Once you do select an agent, you'll want to get preapproved for financing. The process varies depending on the loan product, but the basic idea is that you'll provide any documents relevant to that loan program—typically, proof of your income and assets, personal identi-fication, and more. The lender will use any collected information to determine your eligibility for the loan. If eligible, they will give you a preapproval letter to submit along with any offers to strengthen your standing with the seller.

I'll primarily present loans offering thirty-year terms and fixed interest rates. While investors can succeed with loans that have shorter terms, adjusting interest rates, and balloon payments, longer terms and fixed rates drastically reduce risk when investing because you know exactly what you are signing up for. For this reason, I wouldn't recommend using such risky loan products unless you are an advanced investor.

Owner-Occupied Loans

As previously discussed, house hacking can be a viable option for those willing to live in part of the property while renting out the remaining rooms. It allows you to learn the management ropes "on the job," and more importantly, by occupying the property, you gain access to more desirable loan options. If you don't want to live in the property while renting it, you can still purchase it with an owner-occupied loan. Then, after a year or longer, you can move and begin renting the property out using the co-living strategy while keeping the owner-occupied loan in place.

There are a couple of benefits that all owner-occupied loans share. One advantage is that you can bring a minimal down payment to purchase the property. It is often said that you have to bring 20 percent down to buy real estate. This is not true! If you agree to live in the property for at least one year, it is possible to bring as low as 0% down. Another perk is that the interest rates are superior to those of non-owner-occupied properties. The spread varies, but owner-occupied loans are usually 0.5–1 percent better. That could equate to hundreds of dollars per month in savings.

Owner-occupied loans aren't all sunshine and rainbows, though; some downsides exist. The first one is obvious: You have to live in the property. This can be difficult for someone who already has a family or a lifestyle of living independently. I know married couples with kids who house hack (with separate living spaces, kitchens, bathrooms, and bedrooms), but it can be difficult. Furthermore, your loan amount and monthly payment is higher since you put less down, inhibiting cash flow. In general, putting less down is an excellent idea because you often get higher returns on your investment. However, if putting less down turns your cash flow negative, you now have a negative return on your investment, which is never a good idea. If you find that putting a low amount down causes your cash flow to become negative, you can always put more down until your cash flow reaches an acceptable level, but it diminishes the owner-occupied loan's low-down-payment benefit.

Owner-occupied loans can be an excellent starting place for those with limited cash. This is precisely how my wife and I bought our first two co-living properties. We bought the first one with 5 percent down ($23,000) and lived in it while renting rooms. One year later, we purchased the second one with 5 percent down ($21,500), moved into it, rented out all the rooms at the old place, and rented out some rooms in the new place.

CONVENTIONAL LOANS (OWNER-OCCUPIED)

The most common type of owner-occupied loan is conventional loans, sometimes referred to as Fannie Mae or Freddie Mac loans, available to borrowers with good credit and income.

While you can put 20 percent or more down, smaller down payments are common. You can put down as low as 3 percent if you are a first-time homebuyer, although 5 percent down is typical and offers better terms. If you choose to bring less than 20 percent, you must pay for private mortgage insurance (PMI).

PMI is an additional cost, paid on a monthly or annual basis as part of your mortgage, that protects the lender. With so little money put down, the lender carries a greater risk of losing money if property values decrease or you do not make on-time payments. This is unlikely to happen to you since co-living performs well during recessions when more people need cheaper housing. However, you'll have to pay PMI anyway. The exact cost of PMI varies based on factors such as your credit score and down payment amount, but you can expect the annual PMI to be roughly 0.5 percent of the original loan amount.

Fortunately, with conventional loans, PMI can be removed. Once your loan balance reaches 80 percent of the property value at purchase, you can request that PMI be removed. Alternatively, if you do not make a request, PMI should automatically be removed once the loan balance reaches 78 percent of the original property value. If your property has significantly increased in value, you may want to order an appraisal to determine the new value. If the result shows that your loan amount is 80 percent of the new value, you can get PMI removed even sooner.

FEDERAL HOUSING ADMINISTRATION (FHA) LOANS

FHA loans are available to more borrowers, as the agency has loosened requirements on credit score and income. They allow you to bring as little as 3.5 percent down. However, FHA loans have some downsides you should be aware of.

Property inspection is more stringent and difficult to pass than with conventional loans. In competitive markets, sellers often prefer offers with traditional financing due to the higher likelihood of closing.

Additionally, transitioning from your first house hack to a second one with an FHA loan can present challenges. You'll need to meet additional requirements to use the rental income from your first house hack to qualify for the second, such as having 25 percent equity and being at least one hundred miles from the first property.

Similar to conventional loans, FHA loans require you to pay an extra fee called mortgage insurance premium (MIP). Unlike the PMI on conventional loans, MIP is required no matter how much money you put down. Also, if you put less than 10 percent down, MIP lasts for the life of the loan and cannot be removed without refinancing.

VETERANS AFFAIRS (VA) LOANS

VA loans are exclusively available to active military members and veterans. If you have access to one of these loans, it's an incredible product! It uniquely allows for as low as zero percent down and does not have PMI or MIP. Additionally, the interest rates can be even lower than FHA and conventional while having no official credit requirement (although specific lenders may have requirements in place).

There is a VA funding fee at purchase, however, that can increase your acquisition cost. This fee can be rolled into the loan, but it still adds to the overall cost. Furthermore, VA appraisals and inspections are often stricter than conventional, so in competitive markets, sellers may lean toward conventional offers.

Non-Owner-Occupied Loans

Non-owner-occupied loans are outstanding when you don't want to or cannot live in the property. Generally, you'll have to bring at least 20 percent or 25 percent as a down payment, and the interest rate will be higher than that of owner-occupied loans. While these loans have many variants, let's discuss the two most common ones used for co-living purchases.

CONVENTIONAL LOANS (NON-OWNER-OCCUPIED)

Non-owner-occupied conventional loans are what most investors are referring to when they mention "investor loans."

The interest rate on these loans is usually 0.5–1 percent higher than owner-occupied loans. Also, one borrower is limited to ten conventional loans. Once this limit is met, you'll be denied and have to find another financing source.

Similar to its owner-occupied counterpart, this loan is given based on the quality of the borrower. So, if you were to use one of these loans, the lender wouldn't care about the property as much as they would about your financial situation.

Lenders will evaluate your credit score. You'll likely need a minimum credit score of 620, but the terms improve as the score increases.

Lenders are also interested in your debt-to-income (DTI) ratio. This is your total debt divided by your total income and basically measures if you can handle your debt load. DTI can sometimes be very limiting as you acquire more properties. I've encountered situations where lenders were unwilling to consider co-living income for properties owned for less than two years, but they still counted the debt. So, they increased the numerator while holding the denominator steady, thus overestimating my DTI. Other lenders I've worked with were more willing to use co-living income before I owned the property for two years; so if you encounter this issue, you may need to find a new lender.

Lastly, lenders will investigate your employment status. Conventional lenders prefer borrowers with W-2 income. If you are self-employed, qualifying will be more difficult. Self-employed borrowers usually have to show two years of sufficient income on tax returns to qualify. So if you are recently self-employed or not showing enough W-2 income, you may not quality for conventional investor loans.

DSCR LOANS

Debt service coverage ratio (DSCR) loans are another type of non-owner-occupied loan. When used properly, they can quickly scale your portfolio, but there are some drawbacks.

A considerable benefit of the DSCR loan is that the lender is primarily interested in the property's performance and not you as the borrower. While your credit score is of interest, they do not care about your DTI or your employment status. Instead, they want to know if the property's income will cover the debt (i.e., the mortgage payment). The more the income exceeds the debt, the better the terms of the loan will be. Usually, the income must at least meet the mortgage payment, but some lenders will allow you to have less income than the mortgage payment. I wouldn't recommend that, though. If the property meets the coverage requirement, you should be good to go, although the lender may have other minor requirements.

Another benefit of DSCR loans is that the terms can often be more creative. A common variation of the DSCR that I often use is a ten-year, interest-only option. With this variant, the first ten years of the mortgage payment are interest-only, and the last twenty years of the payment include principal and are amortized over twenty years. While some investors may be hesitant to use an interest-only product, I've found that it is a great way to free up thousands of dollars in cash flow annually. However, this means that I am building less equity in the property.

Equity is calculated as the property value minus the outstanding loan balance. Usually, your property value increases over time, and your loan balance decreases over time, thus increasing your equity. With the interest-only option, your property value will still grow, but your loan balance will remain unchanged, so your equity will build more slowly. Personally, I don't care about trapping equity in my properties. I'd rather have cash that can be smartly reinvested, so I like placing cash in my pocket rather than paying the principal. However, standard principal products are also a great option, and I still use those too.

Unlike conventional loans, you can have as many DSCR loans as you can qualify for. As with most loans, applying for a DSCR loan will temporarily ding your credit since the lender will check your score. The DSCR loan may not be reported to credit agencies, but do your research and double-check this with your lender. I was told that a particular lender wouldn't report the DSCR loan to the credit bureaus. But after closing, I was notified that a new loan had been reported. A few months later, I received some mail saying that the loan was being removed from my credit report due to some lawsuits, so this fortunately isn't an issue anymore.

A downside of DSCR loans is that their rates are higher than those of conventional loans. They are 0.5–1 percent higher than non-owner-occupied conventional loans and 1–2 percent higher than owner-occupied traditional loans, increasing your monthly mortgage payment.

Lastly, DSCR loans often have prepayment penalties. Prepayment penalties are fees incurred if you pay off the loan before the agreed-upon period, usually by selling or refinancing. Commonly, you'll see three-year prepayment penalties. You'll pay 3 percent of the outstanding loan balance as a fee in the first year, a 2 percent fee in the second year, a 1 percent fee in the third year, and no fee afterward. The five-year prepayment penalty works similarly. This is my least favorite part of DSCR loans, as it limits your flexibility. For example, I bought a handful of co-living properties at the end of 2023 at an 8.5 percent interest rate. They cash flow strongly because I'm using the co-living strategy, but I'd love to refinance them at the 6.5 percent rate the market currently offers. Doing so would free up $800 in monthly cash flow on each property. I do have the option to refinance now, but I'll have to pay that hefty fee for doing so. There may be a point where it is worth paying the fee if the interest rate drops low enough, but it still stings!

Seller Financing

Seller financing is a possible option, whether you occupy the property or not. Most commonly, seller financing becomes worth considering when the seller owns the property without a mortgage.

Seller financing is when, instead of getting a loan from a bank to buy the property, you get a loan from the seller and pay them instead. This can be great for some sellers, especially if the property was a rental for them, as they can continue receiving monthly checks as usual without worrying about the hassles of ownership. Additionally, seller financing can help ease the seller's tax burden by spreading the proceeds from the sale over many years rather than paying a huge tax bill all at once.

For you, the buyer, seller financing can prove beneficial since the terms are flexible. Unlike with banks, there are no universal requirements for the loan, so the terms are whatever you and the seller agree to. You may negotiate a lower interest rate and down payment than banks currently offer; however, sellers are rarely willing to offer thirty-year terms. Often, they will want the loan to be paid within three to ten years. Still, you may get fantastic terms for that period and refinance into a bank loan prior to the end of the seller financing period.

You may consider this option if you do not qualify for bank loans due to your credit and income or if the property performance is subpar with other financing options. Henry Washington discusses this method at length in his book *Real Estate Deal Maker* (www.BiggerPockets.com/ReadDealMaker).

Insurance

Insurance is important for any rental property investing strategy. Guidance varies by situation and location, so a professional should be involved. Your real estate agent and lender can give you a list of insurance brokers they've worked with and recommend.

An insurance agent often represents a single insurance company, while an insurance broker represents you and evaluates various insurance companies to find the best policy. I'd recommend using an insurance broker since they have your best interest in mind and provide the most options. Your real estate agent should be able to provide you with references.

Some strategies require specific types of insurance. Short-term rentals, for example, require specialized insurance due to their short-term nature and the number of furnishings within the property.

With co-living, your residents are considered long term, so you may be able to use a standard rental policy rather than a specialized product. Not all companies cover room rentals, but some do. After a lot of searching, my insurance broker has found a handful of companies whose standard policies allow co-living.

If your broker finds the right provider, the plan should cost within 10 percent of a normal policy. I've been hearing more and more about specialized co-living policies that cost twice as much as standard policies. Before resorting to one of these more expensive policies, talk with more brokers to find one who will work diligently to find a standard policy that covers co-living rather than using a specialized policy.

You may want to consider additional coverage for the furnishings you use to outfit the property. In co-living properties, you'll have less-costly furnishings than in short-term rentals, so it could be best to replace the furnishings if damage occurs rather than pay for a policy. However, if you have high-end furnishings, you could find the additional coverage worth the cost.

Still, chat with an insurance broker and get recommendations for your location and situation.

Chapter 5

Finding the Ideal Property

Now that you've selected a market, built out your team, and selected your financing method, it is time to purchase a property ideal for co-living. Not all properties work well for co-living; most of them do not. It may be tempting to convert properties you already own into co-living. This can work occasionally, but often, they won't have enough parking, and you'll feel the need to cram too many people into a layout that will leave the residents feeling uncomfortably packed.

The ideal co-living property is a large house with lots of parking, many bathrooms, and the potential to have more than five bedrooms. We'll discuss further details throughout the chapter to help you find the best home for your residents that produces high cash flow.

The Co-Living Property Funnel

As with selecting a market, it is best to approach the process of finding a property systematically. By using the co-living property funnel seen in Figure 8, you'll be able to ingest hundreds of leads and run them through the various stages of the funnel. At the end, the resulting handful of incredible properties will be solid options for you to add to your portfolio.

For my first two properties, I followed a much more shoot-from-the-hip approach: I glanced through Zillow, walked a few properties, crunched some numbers, and made some offers. This resulted in the purchase of two mediocre properties. Remember, most properties are not suited for co-living!

These days, I have to put 500 leads into the funnel before I close on an excellent co-living property, so when I was glancing through listings willy-nilly, the odds that I'd find that one out of 500 after a few showings were very low.

Therefore, I recommend following a systematic approach that allows you to regularly enter leads, work through the stages, and eventually find great properties.

This chapter will focus on the funnel's upper parts, which involve finding potential deals and filtering out the worst candidates. In Chapter 6: Analyzing and Making Offers, we'll focus on the remaining parts of the funnel.

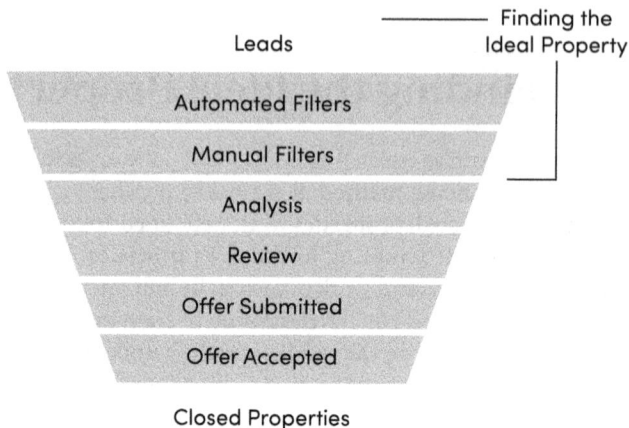

```
                                    ─────── Finding the
                    Leads                    Ideal Property
┌──────────────────────────────────────┐
│          Automated Filters            │
├──────────────────────────────────────┤
│            Manual Filters             │
├──────────────────────────────────────┤
│              Analysis                 │
├──────────────────────────────────────┤
│               Review                  │
├──────────────────────────────────────┤
│           Offer Submitted             │
├──────────────────────────────────────┤
│            Offer Accepted             │
└──────────────────────────────────────┘
                Closed Properties
```

Figure 7. The co-living property funnel

Leads

The first step is to find leads to add to the top of the funnel. A lead is simply any property with an owner who wishes to sell. You can find such leads on or off market.

On-Market Leads

On-market leads are the easiest to find. Most owners who wish to sell their property hire a real estate agent and list their property on the market, also known as the Multiple Listings Service (MLS). Simply put the MLS is a repository of all properties sold through real estate agents. Historically, the only way to know what properties were on this list was to hire your agent and have the listings relayed to you. These days, it is much simpler.

Websites like Zillow, Redfin, and Realtor.com are clones of the MLS that anyone can view. When you sign up to work with a real estate agent they will likely ask you questions about the type of property you are looking for and offer to set you up with MLS notifications. This can be useful, as their MLS portal sometimes provides access to filters that the clones do not have, but I often decline their offer and instead use Zillow.

Searching Zillow offers many benefits. First, Zillow has developed features unavailable with raw MLS data. They have estimates regarding property value, video walk-throughs of the property, summaries of nearby attractions, and property tax history. Similar to your agent's notifications, you can set up alerts to get notified when new properties are listed from Zillow.

Now that you know where you can find on-market leads, you need to choose where to receive them: directly from your agent or from an MLS clone. Regardless, you'll want to receive email notifications instantly when a new property is listed or in a daily summary. When the market was very hot in 2022, I signed up for instant notifications since submitting an offer for properties within two hours of listing was a must. Now that things have cooled off, I receive daily reports instead.

Next, you'll need to store these leads somewhere so you can put them through the stages of the funnel. A simple spreadsheet including the address, square footage, bedroom and bathroom count, asking price, and a link to the property will suffice. Alternatively, you can just make a list with pen and paper. Don't overwhelm yourself with storing a ton of information at this point. You can evolve your process to include more or less data over time, but this serves as a good start.

Off-Market Leads

Off-market leads are a whole other can of worms and involve additional work to find. Off-market leads are properties whose owners have identified that they want to sell but haven't listed their property with an agent yet. There could be many reasons for this. They may need to sell quickly, and involving an agent can slow that process down. The property may be in poor condition, so a traditional homebuyer would be uninterested in the home if it were listed.

Off-market leads can often have better returns, as you can purchase them at lower prices due to less competition. Finding these leads is best described in *Real Estate Deal Maker* by Henry Washington (www.BiggerPockets.com/ReadDealMaker). Alternatively, you can have off-market leads delivered to you by wholesalers; just be prepared to pay in exchange for the work they perform.

Once you have identified off-market leads, you can store the property information in the same way as on-market properties.

Since high-cash-flowing co-living properties can be found on the market, that is the lead source I have exclusively pursued; however, if your superpower is talking and negotiating with potential sellers and managing remodels of distressed properties, then this can be a way to boost your returns even more.

Automated Filters

Now that you have leads entering the funnel, you want to be smart about the order in which you push them through it. For example, time-consuming and manual tasks like looking at Google Street View to evaluate the parking situation are wastes of time if the property isn't even in the part of town you like, so screen out as many properties as possible with automatic filters first.

There are two different approaches to filtering. The first option is to combine the leads and automated filtering steps by just filtering with Zillow. Instead of putting every listing into your funnel, you only enter the ones Zillow has already filtered for you. Alternatively, you can enter every unfiltered lead from Zillow into the funnel and perform the filters yourself. I prefer the latter method. I want to know exactly how many listings need to hit the market for the funnel to produce a deal. This is probably overkill for most investors, so combining the leads and automated filters step is also acceptable.

You can apply many automated filters, but I'll just present some of the most common ones.

Location

As with all real estate strategies, location is a significant factor in a property's performance. Perhaps you are willing to purchase anywhere in the city you've selected, but typically, you'll want to filter further, into zip codes and neighborhoods.

The most crucial factor when refining the location is proximity to places your target demographic visits. If you intend to rent to students, purchase near a university. If you want to rent to military members, purchase near a military base. If you plan to rent to low-income earners, young professionals, or traveling workers, purchase near their places of employment. How close you need to be to these locations varies. At the university I attended, most students wanted to live within a fifteen-minute walk to their classes. At other universities, students may be willing to drive fifteen minutes. Some dense cities may have young professionals accustomed to walking five minutes to their tech jobs downtown. Other towns may have young professionals willing to drive thirty minutes to work. You'll have to dig into the city and chat with your target demographic to determine these specifics.

Once you've determined how far you want to be from certain points of interest, you can draw a boundary on the map in Zillow and save it to your saved search. You can also filter by zip code and neighborhood.

HOA

Homeowner associations (HOAs) create and enforce rules over a community, often at the neighborhood level. If you buy a property within one of these neighborhoods, you are usually required to become a member of the HOA, pay dues to support its efforts, and abide by its rules. An HOA aims to maintain the condition of the neighborhood by setting standards and building or maintaining amenities like clubhouses and swimming pools. This sounds great, but you'll also be subject to restrictions that can negatively affect the co-living strategy.

For starters, HOAs have the power to require that the owner lives in the property, preventing the property from being rented out. Further, even if an HOA allows renters, it can limit the number of renters. Rules can be written as "no more than X people allowed to live in the home," but more often, parking restrictions limit the number of renters. Many HOAs have rules that cars cannot be parked on the street overnight. This effectively limits the number of renters to the number of garage spots you have, unless you are in a very walkable area where most renters don't have cars.

If these regulations aren't enough, HOA fees can increase out of your control, and you must pay them. I know an investor who owns a condo within an HOA community. This community is prone to damaging hailstorms, so the HOA had an insurance policy that should have covered roof replacements. A storm rolled through, damaging the roof. Although a portion of the HOA dues had been allocated to paying for this insurance policy, the HOA discovered that they had purchased a policy that would not cover any of the damage. So, a special assessment of $10,000/person was required to replace the roof without insurance. The community was mostly made up of older folks on social security who struggled to find that much cash on such short notice. They had little choice, however, as the consequence was the HOA placing a lien on their property.

Because of the lack of property control and fees, I categorically avoid HOAs. State and city regulatory bodies can already create laws and ordinances that affect your portfolio, so why add another governing body that is out of your control? Even if I were to read the HOA rules and find out that no restrictions exist that would affect my co-living property, I'd still avoid purchasing a property there. Once the HOA discovers that you have five-plus residents at the property, they can create occupancy or parking rules that will turn your cash-flowing property into a hole in your pocket.

Property Type

Next, you can filter based on property type: single-family homes, condos, townhomes, and small multifamily homes (duplex, triplex, fourplex). You may choose one or multiple types to pursue. When choosing between the types, consider these factors: appreciation, control, price, and location.

SINGLE-FAMILY HOMES

Single-family homes tend to appreciate more than other property types since they are desirable to the largest pool of buyers: families. They also tend to be the most desirable to co-living residents, as they look the best in listing photos due to their curb appeal and large yards that alternative options usually lack. Additionally, you have greater control over the asset's use (unless it's part of an HOA) as you own the land and the house. Purchase price tends to run in the middle of the pack; single-family homes are more expensive than townhomes and condos but less expensive than small multifamily properties. Lastly, they can be located in good or bad parts of town, so talk to your agent and locals to understand the specifics.

CONDOS AND TOWNHOMES

Condos and townhomes tend to appreciate less than single-family homes; however, they have a lower purchase price and barrier to entry. Additionally, they are usually in excellent parts of town where room rental residents would like to live. They typically have HOAs, however, so I wouldn't recommend investing in them.

SMALL MULTIFAMILY HOMES

Small multifamily properties may appreciate less than single-family homes, but they can have more square footage, providing opportunities for more rooms. HOAs are rare, so parking and other regulations are less of an issue than with condos and townhomes. However, be sure to check the location of small multifamily properties. In many markets I've evaluated, multifamily properties are confined to certain parts of town due to zoning, which tend to be more run-down and less desirable for residents. This is not always the case, so do your research.

Property Size

Co-living is a strategy that produces more cash flow the larger the properties are. Would having six or more residents even be reasonable, or is that a landlord's selfish attempt to boost cash flow? As long as the property layout comfortably supports additional bedrooms, I've found that more bedrooms are actually better for the community. Recently, I asked the residents of my eight-bedroom rental if they had made any friends in the house. They said that four of them interact regularly, while the others keep to themselves. If this were a five-bedroom house, it would be difficult for the community to develop, as only two or three of them would probably socialize.

In Table 4, you can see six different property sizes with an increasing number of bedrooms. Assuming the rooms rent for $800 each and that properties cost $180 per square foot, you can see the different-sized properties' annual income and purchase price. Lastly, you can find the rent-to-price ratio. Similar to the rent-to-price ratio you calculated in the market analysis section, this number describes the bang you are getting for your buck.

Sq. Ft.	Bedrooms	Annual Rent	Price	Rent/Price
1,800	5	$48,000	$324,000	14.81%
2,050	6	$57,600	$369,000	15.61%
2,250	7	$67,200	$405,000	16.59%
2,500	8	$76,800	$450,000	17.07%
2,750	9	$86,400	$495,000	17.45%
3,000	10	$96,000	$540,000	17.78%

Table 4. Rent/price ratio by varying property size

As you can see, the bang for your buck grows as the property size increases because the property layout becomes more efficient. When you have a five-bedroom house, you have one kitchen and one living room. When you have a ten-bedroom house, you still have one kitchen and one living room. So, while the kitchen and living room size is fixed, all additional square footage directly contributes to more space for bedrooms and thus more income.

For this reason, the larger the property the better. However, this doesn't mean you should only filter to 3,000-square-foot houses. Most markets do not have many properties that size, so if you applied such a filter, you would have very few leads to sift through. Instead, you want to balance property size while maintaining decent lead flow.

In 2024's interest rate and purchase price environment, I typically see cash flow become sufficient at the six-bedroom mark, so I filter for 2,050 square feet and up, but this has changed over time. When I purchased my first property, prices and interest rates were lower, and cash flow was adequate at the five-bedroom mark. Initially, I'd recommend leaving the property filter size less restrictive, and as you analyze more properties and become more familiar with the market, you can tighten up this filter. For reference, my portfolio's smallest and largest properties are 2,200 square feet and 3,300 square feet respectively.

Counterintuitively, you should never filter on bedroom count. As I've mentioned, the more bedrooms, the better, though there is one problem: six-, seven-, eight-, nine-, or ten-bedroom houses rarely exist! If you want incredible cash flow, you must create these houses by adding bedrooms. You shouldn't be concerned with how many bedrooms a home has when you purchase it. Instead, during your analysis, you'll include the appropriate remodel budget to add the number of bedrooms the property can comfortably support.

Manual Filters

Now that you've quickly filtered out all properties that don't meet the location, HOA, property type, and property size requirements you've set, you need to manually investigate the remaining candidates further.

Parking

Parking can make or break a co-living property but takes little time to check for. Parking is imperative, as you may have six to ten vehicles for residents at a single property. Critics of this strategy often point out that the number of cars can burden the rest of the neighborhood, which is a valid concern. If someone else's residents routinely parked in front of my house, blocking my mailbox and making it difficult for my visitors to park, I would probably be frustrated too. I don't want the investors reading this book to be the ones who give co-living a bad reputation by ruining the neighborhood experience for homeowners. Instead, be mindful of the parking situation and only select the properties with the best parking to minimize friction in the neighborhood.

First, let's discuss how many parking spots are needed. If you have eight residents, you need eight parking places, right? Sometimes you might, but it is dependent on the city. For example, my market is pretty spread out and doesn't have a good public transport system, so nearly 100 percent of my residents have cars. In this case, I want no less than one parking spot for every resident. In other markets with excellent public transportation, residents have the ability to take that transport to work, so you may only need parking for four residents.

A great way to calculate the parking you'll need is with walkscore.com. You can directly go to this website, or view the scores included at the bottom of Zillow listings. If you type in a zip code or the specific address of a property, it will return a walk, transit, and bike score. The transit score is most useful to co-living residents, as they may use public transport to travel to work and other local destinations. The higher the score, the better access this location has to buses, trains, and ferries. Once you have this score, you can use Table 5 to estimate the parking spots you need.

Transit Score Range	Parking Spots per Resident
90–100 (Rider's paradise)	0.25
70–89 (Good transit)	0.5
50–69 (Some transit)	0.75
25–49 (Minimal transit)	1
0–24 (No transit)	1

Table 5. Parking spots needed for co-living based on transit scores from walkscore.com

What constitutes a parking spot though? If your potential properties are in a downtown environment where street parking in front of other people's houses is the norm, anywhere could be considered a parking spot—but make certain that this is true. Co-living properties are frequently purchased in neighborhoods, where this is not the case. If you are in a neighborhood where you think there is even a tiny chance of a neighbor complaining about your residents' parking, you'll need a well-thought-out parking plan.

I have not always been so diligent about parking. My first house hack was in an area where parking on the street seemed to be the norm and widely accepted. When my wife and I saw a listing for this house with a one-car garage and frontage long enough for two more cars, we thought we were golden. Eventually, I filled the property with five residents, and a couple of vehicles now needed to park elsewhere. This seemed to work until I had to park in front of a particular neighbor's house across the street. This neighbor was the only one who actively cared for his property, often working on his flower beds and lawn.

With the available spots at my house occupied, I had to park in front of his house. Once I got through my front door, I glanced out a window and spotted him looking at my truck, trying to identify whose vehicle it was. I continued along with my day thinking nothing of it. A couple of days later, when I returned to my truck, I noticed the decals on my tailgate had been pried off and left on the ground. Obviously, he hadn't liked where I parked, but I thought this was an anomaly and didn't learn my lesson.

As our next house hack, we purchased a property with insufficient parking. Once the property was fully occupied, one resident had to park across the street in front of a neighbor's house. The neighbor knocked on the door and asked if that was my car. I replied, "That is my roommate's car. We live with a few guys because it's hard to afford a mortgage these days." He sympathized, but that conversation would have gone differently if I, as the owner, hadn't lived there and it were purely an investment property.

Using Google Street View, you can determine if a property will have enough parking, but what areas can be considered parking spots? In Figure 9, you'll find all of the types of parking I look for. A property doesn't need to have every option—it just needs to have enough.

Garage spaces and the driveway in front of them are obvious possibilities (Label 1). A two-car garage can count as two spots, a three-car garage can count as three, etc. Remember that you cannot count the driveway spots in addition to the garage spots. For the residents to be able to back out of the garage, the driveway must be empty.

Parking pads and portions of the driveway that do not block the garage can also be considered for parking (Label 2).

Any parking along the front and sides of the property can be considered as well (Labels 3-1 and 3-2). Corner lots are often great contenders because they often have an abundance of parking along the side. Be conservative when counting how many cars can parallel park along the property, as residents may not pack their cars in as tightly as you may assume.

You may also consider the side yards of nearby properties, especially if they have a fence (Label 4). I've never had a neighbor complain when parked along their side fence. The key is to *never* park in front of a neighbor's house.

Figure 8. Parking example for co-living

Be creative! Consider building additional parking. Perhaps you can add a gravel or concrete pad in the yard for additional cars.

Bedroom and Bathroom Additions

Remember how you ignored the current number of bedrooms when doing the automated filtering? The name of the co-living game is adding bedrooms. Especially in a high-price, high-interest-rate environment, properties rarely cash flow sufficiently with the existing number of bedrooms. You must wear your creativity hat once again and discern where to add bedrooms. You can use Table 6 to estimate how many bedrooms you may have based on the property size. These estimates are based on my actual portfolio.

You can see that a 2,500-square-foot property can support up to eight bedrooms if it has the right layout. This is the best-case scenario. I have a 2,500-square-foot property with eight bedrooms because it has a smaller kitchen and living room with little unused space. I have other properties that are 3,200 square feet and also have eight bedrooms. The living room and kitchen are large at these properties, and office or flex spaces are too small to make into bedrooms. Referencing this table can give you a starting point for the ideal number of bedrooms you could add, but you'll need to dive deeper to get a more accurate estimate.

Property sq. ft.	Maximum # of Bedrooms
1,800	5
2,050	6
2,250	7
2,500	8
2,750	9
3,000	10

Table 6. Maximum number of bedrooms for various property sizes

After referencing the table to see how many bedrooms you can achieve, reference the listing photos to find the spaces that can be converted. Sometimes, you'll find 3D walk-throughs and floor plans attached to the listing, speeding this process along. In some markets, the county or city's property accessor and permitting websites may have floor plans available for you. In my market, the floor plans are accessible for a $20/month subscription, which has been worth the cost. It can be challenging to determine where rooms can be added from the pictures alone, but paying for the floor plans has allowed me to get a better idea of this without sending my agent to the house for a tour.

The definition of a bedroom can vary from market to market, so be sure to search your city, county, and state definitions. Generally, a bedroom requires two forms of egress, a closet, a locking entry door, HVAC vents, and suitable floor space. You'll learn more about these requirements in Chapter 7: Remodeling.

When you look through the listing photos and floor plan, suitable bedroom conversion opportunities include offices, dining rooms, sitting rooms, extra living rooms, family rooms, game rooms, flex spaces, and large basements (finished or unfinished).

If the property can support eight rooms but you find that it only has enough parking for a property with six residents, you'll want to reduce the number of rooms to six. Remember, you don't want to exceed the parking limit you determined and cause issues in the neighborhood. Keep a tally of the number of bedrooms that can be added, as you'll need it for the property analysis.

Now that you know the number of bedrooms the property could have, you can determine how many bathrooms are required. A good rule of thumb is three people or less to a bathroom with a shower or tub, sink, and toilet. Fewer residents to a bathroom will reduce conflict and increase rents and desirability. The best way to increase the number of bathrooms is by expanding half bathrooms (bathrooms with a sink and toilet only) to add a shower stall or shower/tub combo. I sometimes build bathrooms from scratch, but existing half baths have all the plumbing needed and are much more cost effective to convert.

Keep in mind the number of bathrooms that can be converted or built from scratch. You'll need this for the property analysis.

Here is a video of how I investigated the floor plan of an actual property to determine how many bedrooms and bathrooms could be added: www.BiggerPockets.com/CoLivingBonus.

Chapter 6

Analyzing and Making Offers

By this point, you've filtered the leads down to properties that have the potential to be great for co-living. Do the numbers make sense, and can you secure the deal? That is what we will focus on with the remaining steps of the funnel.

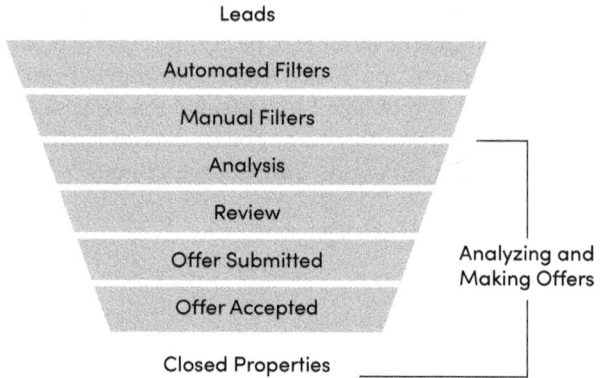

Leads

Automated Filters

Manual Filters

Analysis

Review

Offer Submitted

Analyzing and
Making Offers

Offer Accepted

Closed Properties

Figure 9. The co-living property funnel

Analysis

You knew this was coming: the property analysis! At this stage, you'll crunch all the property details and determine how profitable all the remaining leads are.

Determining Your Performance Requirements

How will you know if a lead is a good deal worth purchasing? You should set minimum criteria that the property must meet. I am a stickler, but if a property falls short of your requirements, even by 1 percent, I wouldn't recommend buying it. That is why I call them requirements and not goals. If you are short by a smidge, renegotiate with the seller and find out how to achieve that last bit of performance. Define your rules for buying, and stick to them as if they were law.

The first thing to consider when determining your requirements is what you want your co-living properties to do for you. Refer to the market goals you set earlier, but now dive deeper. Do you want cash flow now to quit your job, even if it means getting less appreciation and long-term wealth? Are you comfortable with your current income and just want a property that pays for itself and eventually is sold for massive profit in twenty years? Do you want to assume the risk of high leverage if it means you may receive better returns? Do you wish to pay off your property within five years to reduce risk, retire, and supercharge your cash flow? Questions like these should be deeply pondered for at least an hour. Include your significant other if you have one.

Once you know how you want your co-living portfolio to affect your life, choose some performance metrics that can measure that effect. I recommend reading *Real Estate by the Numbers* by J Scott and Dave Meyer (www.BiggerPockets.com/ReadBytheNumbers) to fully understand the different metrics that measure a property's performance, but these are a good starting point:

- Cash flow: the profit from the property after all expenses are paid
- Cash-on-cash return: the amount of cash you receive in your pocket for every dollar you invest
- Appreciation: the increase in property value over time, often exceeding cash flow, though it remains trapped as equity and cannot be readily accessed
- Net operating income (NOI): the cash flow generated by the property if purchased without a loan or after the loan is fully paid off
- Cap rate: the amount of cash you receive in your pocket for every dollar you invest if purchased without a loan or after the loan is fully paid off
- Internal rate of return (IRR): a comprehensive measure of how hard each dollar you invest works, factoring in cash flow, appreciation, and other returns, while accounting for the time value of money

I am mainly building my co-living portfolio to produce income that my family can use to pay for our personal expenses. Any appreciation will be the cherry on top when I eventually sell, but it isn't my main concern. For this reason, I focus on two metrics: cash flow and cash-on-cash return.

I require the property to produce $2,000 per month in cash flow. This is unique to my situation because I invest with partners with whom I split the cash flow. Ultimately, I want to take home $1,000 per month for myself. Therefore, I need double that. If I were an investor who didn't use partners, perhaps I would only require the property to produce $1,000 per month.

Additionally, I require that the property have a 12 percent cash-on-cash return or greater because I want a much higher return than investing passively in the stock market. 12 percent is hard but achievable to find in my market so when I do find it, I know it is a stellar deal. If I were in a different market that offered 12 percent cash-on-cash more easily, perhaps I would require 16 percent.

Don't forget that you can adjust your performance requirements over time. Some investors advise against this, but your goals change.

There may come a point where my co-living portfolio is generating much more cash flow than I need. At that point, I may want to focus more on appreciation and building long-term wealth. Alternatively, market conditions may change. If property prices fall drastically and I can easily get 18 percent cash-on-cash returns, you better believe I will shoot for 25 percent returns and pass on all the 12 percent returns I previously targeted.

Be careful and ensure that the deal is still a deal if you change your requirements. Don't lower your requirements to the point that the juice isn't worth the squeeze.

Running the Numbers

Now that you have defined your performance requirements, you can run the numbers on the leads left in your funnel.

The goal isn't to determine whether this property meets your performance requirements at its asking price. Instead, the goal is to determine the purchase price needed to achieve your performance requirements. This may sound like a subtle difference, but it has enabled me to purchase many properties for less than the asking price.

For example, a property I looked at was listed for $600,000. I ran the analysis at that purchase price, and it yielded negative cash flow, even with eight rooms. Did that stop me? No! I varied the purchase price and found that at $525,000, it met my performance requirements. I repeatedly made that offer over many weeks, and eventually, the seller accepted.

You must select a reliable tool that will accurately run the numbers for you, rather than relying on a desk calculator or running the numbers in your head. After all, you are deploying hundreds of thousands of dollars of your hard-earned money. Don't let a simple math mistake ruin your investment. In this book, I won't teach how each metric is calculated. Instead, I recommend using a vetted tool like the BiggerPockets Rental Property Calculator (www.BiggerPockets.com/BookRPC). We'll talk more about the best tools in Chapter 14: Tools and Resources.

While tool selection is essential, understanding the inputs for the tool is of equal importance. If you feed a tool garbage inputs, it will give you garbage outputs. The inputs that I present are not an exhaustive list, as I don't discuss common inputs for all investment types, like down payments, principal, interest, etc. Any good calculator will define these and help you calculate them. Instead, I've chosen to focus on the analysis inputs that have a unique co-living twist.

RENT

The rent produced by a co-living property should be much higher than that of a traditional long-term rental. In Chapter 5: Selecting a Market, you determined what a standard room that shares a bathroom would likely rent for as part of the room rental demand test. Rooms that share a bathroom will make up most of the rental income. However, the rooms with a private bathroom will also command more money and be in higher demand because of the added privacy. On average, these primary bedrooms rent for 20 percent higher than the rooms with shared baths. So, when you add up the total rent from all the bedrooms, assuming a 20 percent increase for those rooms is reasonable.

Additionally, depending on the property, you may generate income from more than just room rent. We'll discuss this more in Chapter 13: Ongoing Management, but you can often rent the garage and storage space, so include any additional income you plan to collect.

UTILITIES

Unlike a long-term rental where the tenant pays for all utilities, it is customary for the landlord of a co-living property to pay for all utilities, although it is not required. In Chapter 13: Ongoing Management, we'll discuss the utility options, including paying the utilities yourself and billing the residents back for utilities.

If you decide to pay for utilities, you'll pay for water, sewer, gas, electricity, trash, and even internet.

The water, sewer, gas, and electricity costs will be higher than those of the typical single-family home, as you'll have more people in the house. Table 7 illustrates the usage for each utility type as compared to that of the typical home.

Utility Type	Increased Usage
Gas	10–20%
Water/Sewer	40–100%
Electric	5–50%

Table 7. Utility usage for a co-living property

I created a table with rules of thumb for how much each utility increases for each additional bedroom. I found that the data in my portfolio swung wildly and didn't exactly correlate with the number of residents. For example, I discovered that a five-resident property used 100 percent more water than the typical house, while an eight-resident property only used 40 percent more. This is because some residents are more conservative with utility usage than others.

The provided table is still handy when estimating utility costs. You'll first need to know the average price of each utility in your zip code or city. You can check the provider's website, which may have a breakdown of a typical bill. If it doesn't, you can call the provider and ask how much you could expect to pay. Once you know how much each utility usually costs, I'd be conservative and use the higher end of the estimates in the table.

This is only an estimate, so consider adding a buffer if the forecast is too conservative.

INCOME-SCALED EXPENSES

Income-scaled expenses adjust based on the rent collected. A classic example is repairs and maintenance. In most calculators, you'll see the estimate for this expense as a percentage of the income. Scaling this expense with the property's income is usually a great approach, as properties that generate more income likely have more toilets to maintain, higher-end finishes to repair, etc.

Repairs and Maintenance

As mentioned, repairs and maintenance are great candidates for estimates based on income. When analyzing long-term rentals, expect to use 10 percent of the revenue as an estimate for repairs and maintenance. 10 percent is overkill for a co-living property. In many cases, you'll find that a co-living property will generate two to three times the income that a traditional long-term rental will, but it doesn't need two to three times the repairs. Yes, there will be more wear and tear because of the increased number of inhabitants, but not to that extent.

Based on data from my portfolio, repairs are 2–8 percent of the income, depending on the year. To be conservative, I assume the top end of the range in my analyses.

Capital Expenditures

Capital expenditures, such as replacing the roof or water heater, are often estimated based on income. 10 percent is a standard estimate to use when analyzing long-term rentals. Once again, this is overkill for co-living. Producing two to three times the income doesn't mean the roof or HVAC will wear out two to three times faster. Some systems, like the water heater, may wear out quicker, but not much.

Capital expenditures like the roof need to be replaced over a long period of time. My portfolio doesn't yet have enough data to reliably calculate a percentage based on income. Long-term rental owners generally estimate 10 percent for capital expenditures. Assuming that a co-living property produces double the income and capital expenses occur 50 percent sooner, 7.5 percent of the income is a reasonable estimate. This is what I use in my analyses.

Vacancy

Vacancy can be described as a percentage of the income. As an experienced co-living operator, I strive to maintain 5 percent vacancy or less. This is roughly equivalent to a six-person house with four room turnovers in a year, each lasting four weeks. As a new investor in the co-living strategy, a 10 percent vacancy assumption would be a safer bet. In your first couple of years, you will likely work out the kinks in your marketing and management so you can quickly find residents and retain them, but this will take experience and refinement of your systems.

START-UP COSTS

While the important analysis items we've discussed thus far recur regularly, such as rent, utilities, and income-scaled expenses, there are some costs you'll only incur when you first purchase the property. Examples include your down payment and closing costs. You'll incur these when purchasing any type of property, but there are some co-living-specific initial costs that you should be aware of and include in your analysis.

Furnishing Costs

In a co-living property, you will undoubtedly be furnishing the common areas, such as the living room and kitchen. You may decide to furnish the bedrooms as well. In Chapter 8: Furnishing, we will discuss furnishings in great detail.

Assuming you furnish only the shared spaces, as of the writing of this book in 2025, you'll spend around $5,000. Inflation will increase this cost in the future, so consider adjusting this figure by about 3 percent for each year that has passed since 2025.

Assuming you also furnish the bedrooms, you may add $1,000 for each. Inflate this figure as needed.

Remodel Costs

During the initial property analysis, you'll just want a decent estimate of what the remodel will cost. A rough estimate will suffice at this stage, so there is no need to have contractors walk it yet. Remember, most leads will not reach the bottom of the funnel, so asking them to tour every property you analyze is a waste of time.

In Table 8, you'll find the estimates I use in 2025. I don't recommend using these directly, as these costs will increase over time and vary by market. I'd recommend building a table similar to the one below for yourself by talking with a few contractors.

Item	Cost (Labor + Materials)
Build Bedroom	$3,000
Convert Half Bath	$6,000
Build New Bath	$10,000
Add Egress Window	$7,000

Table 8. Estimates for common co-living remodel items

Initial Reserves

Along with the funds you'll need to furnish and remodel the property, you'll also need some initial reserves. It may take two to three months to achieve a fully occupied property. During this period, you won't have rental income to help pay the mortgage, utilities, and other holding costs. Instead, you'll need cash in the bank to pay these expenses until your rents can cover them. You'll feel a tremendous peace of mind knowing you have cash in the bank, and you don't have to accept a less desirable applicant so you can make the first few mortgage payments.

I like to set aside three months of the mortgage payment for the initial reserves, so I include that in the initial cash needed for the analysis.

Once the property is stabilized, I use the cash flow to replenish the reserve account with three months' worth of mortgage payments. Only then do I start taking cash flow distributions from the property to fund my lifestyle or future investments.

OPTIONAL EXPENSES

Depending on how you decide to run your co-living operations, there may be some other expenses you want to include. We'll talk more about these optional expenses in Chapter 13: Ongoing Management, but I'll list them here so you can include them in your analysis if you wish.

- Lawn care ($40–$120/month)
- House cleaning ($100–$220/month)
- Shared supplies ($50–$80/month)

Analysis Examples

Here is an example analysis of an actual property in my portfolio similar to something you could purchase. While the exact inputs will vary depending on your market, this analysis serves as inspiration for what co-living returns can do for your financial situation.

I purchased this property as a non-owner-occupied investment. You can find the inputs and results in Table 9 and Table 10.

As we've discussed, co-living is a viable strategy for owner-occupied investments also. The returns are quite different, as the mortgage payment and down payment requirements are different, so I'll also show what the same property would produce if bought with an owner-occupied loan in Table 11 and Table 12.

NON-OWNER-OCCUPIED EXAMPLE

Inputs

Acquisition/Startup	
Purchase Price	$472,500
Interest Rate	7.0% (DSCR, 10-year interest-only)
Down Payment	25% ($118,125)
Closing/Loan Costs	$12,496 (includes $6,000 seller credit)
Reserve Account Funding	$7,598 (3x mortgage payment)
Startup Costs	$36,000 ($25,000 for remodel, $5,000 for furnishings, 20% buffer)
Total Investment	$174,219
Income	
Bedrooms with Private Bath (2x)	$1,900/month ($950/month each)
Bedrooms with Shared Bath (6x)	$4,620/month ($770/month each)
Garage Space (2x)	$240/month ($120/month each)
Storage Shed (1x)	$50/month
Gross Monthly Income	$6,810/month
Expenses	
Property Taxes and Insurance	$466/month
Internet	$70/month
Utilities	$296/month
Garbage	$31/month
Landscaping	$42/month
Repairs and Maintenance	$545/month (8%)
Cleaning	$120/month
Vacancy	$341/month (5%)
Interest	$2,067/month
Capital Expenditures	$511/month (7.5%)
Gross Monthly Expenses	$4,489/month

Table 9. Inputs for a non-owner-occupied co-living property

Results

Cash Flow	
Monthly Income	$6,810
Monthly Expenses	$4,489
Monthly Cash Flow	$2,321
Total Annual Cash Flow	$27,852
Investment	$174,219
Cash Flow ROI (Cash-on-Cash Return)	15.99%
Appreciation	
Forced Appreciation	$20,000
Natural Appreciation	$25,220 (4.7%)
Total Annual Appreciation	$45,220
Investment	$174,219
Appreciation ROI	25.96%
Loan Paydown	
Total Annual Principal Paid	$0
Investment	$174,219
Loan Paydown ROI	0.00%
Tax Benefits	
Standard Depreciation	$13,122
Effective Tax Rate	25%
Total Annual Tax Benefit	$3,281
Investment	$174,219
Tax Benefits ROI	1.88%
Total Returns	
Total Annual Return	$76,353
Investment	$174,219
Total ROI	43.83%

Table 10. Results for a non-owner-occupied co-living property

The results show this property generated a 16 percent cash-on-cash return with $2,300 monthly cash flow in the first year! How impactful would that be to your life? Meanwhile, most investors in this market were buying negatively cash-flowing, traditional, long-term rentals. This level of cash flow is totally worth the management headache, in my opinion.

You can observe that by adding all of the various returns (cash flow, appreciation, loan paydown, and tax benefits), this property effectively produced $76,000 and 44 percent ROI in the first year. While I find this impressive, I prefer to focus on cash flow, because the purpose of my portfolio is to provide cash that my family can live on.

OWNER-OCCUPIED (HOUSE HACK) EXAMPLE

Inputs

Acquisition/Startup	
Purchase Price	$472,500
Interest Rate	6.0% (Conventional Loan)
Down Payment	5% ($23,625)
Closing/Loan Costs	$14,953 (includes $6,000 seller credit)
Reserve Account Funding	$9,470 (3x mortgage payment)
Startup Costs	$36,000 ($25,000 for remodel, $5,000 for furnishings, 20% buffer)
Total Investment	$84,048
Income	
Primary Bedroom (2x)	$1,900/month ($950/month each)
Bedrooms with Shared Bath (6x)	$4,620/month ($770/month each)
Garage Space (2x)	$240/month ($120/month each)
Storage Shed (1x)	$50/month
Gross Monthly Income	$6,810/month

Expenses	
Property Taxes and Insurance	$466/month
Internet	$70/month
Utilities	$296/month
Garbage	$31/month
Landscaping	$42/month
Repairs and Maintenance	$545/month (8%)
Cleaning	$120/month
Vacancy	$341/month (5%)
PMI	$221/month
Principal and Interest	$2,691/month
Capital Expenditures	$511/month (7.5%)
Gross Monthly Expenses	$5,334/month

Table 11. Inputs for an owner-occupied co-living property

Results

Cash Flow	
Monthly Income	$6,810
Monthly Expenses	$5,334
Monthly Cash Flow	$1,476
Total Annual Cash Flow	$17,712
Investment	$84,048
Cash Flow ROI (Cash-on-Cash Return)	21.07%
Appreciation	
Forced Appreciation	$20,000
Natural Appreciation	$25,220 (4.7%)
Total Annual Appreciation	$45,220
Investment	$84,048
Appreciation ROI	53.80%
Loan Paydown	
Total Annual Principal Paid	$5,512
Investment	$84,048
Loan Paydown ROI	6.56%
Tax Benefits	
Standard Depreciation	$13,122
Effective Tax Rate	25%
Total Annual Tax Benefit	$3,281
Investment	$84,048
Tax Benefits ROI	3.90%
Total Returns	
Total Annual Return	$71,725
Investment	$84,048
Total ROI	85.34%

Table 12. Results for an owner-occupied co-living property

In the house hack example, cash flow is $1,476/month, a 21 percent cash-on-cash return. The total return is $72,000, 85 percent ROI, in the first year. Imagine purchasing such a profitable property!

Notably, this assumes you've already moved from the property but kept the owner-occupied loan in place. While you live there, the cash flow will obviously decrease as you occupy a portion of the property.

The comparison of these two scenarios is interesting. The cash flow is less for the non-owner-occupied scenario. While the interest rate is 1 percent lower than the non-owner-occupied example, it includes principal payments, whereas the non-owner-occupied example included only interest. The loan balance is also higher for the house hack example because only 5 percent was put down. Therefore, the house hack example has a larger mortgage payment. You'll also see that private mortgage insurance (PMI) reduces the cash flow, as it is required by lenders if you put down less than 20 percent.

While the cash flow is lower, the cash-on-cash return is higher, meaning you are getting more bang for your buck. You require much less money when using an owner-occupied loan, $84,000 instead of $174,000. You are making fewer dollars, but you put far fewer dollars into the deal.

If you want to house hack and are discouraged by the $84,000 needed in this example, there are plenty of properties that require less remodeling. If you found a property that only needed two additional bedrooms, the total funds required could be reduced to $60,000.

Keep in mind that when you hear about the returns of house hacks on social media, they rarely include initial reserves, repairs and maintenance, capital expenditures, etc. The analysis I presented is all encompassing so as to not mislead you.

Review

At this funnel stage, you have applied automatic and manual filters. For leads that pass, you have a purchase price that will allow the investment to meet your performance requirements. Now let's review the property details and reinforce your decision to make an offer.

Gut Check

This isn't mathematical, but I like to perform a gut check by looking through the property pictures and walking through the neighborhood on Google Street View once more. The goal is to confirm that once this property is remodeled and occupied, it will be a place where the residents feel at home. It is difficult to explain, but I'll either feel good (usually) or bad (sometimes) about the lead. I'd never recommend buying a property that gives you a bad feeling just because the numbers make sense. You should feel excited and confident that this property will be an excellent home for your residents and a cash cow for you.

Property Tour

Assuming the property passes my gut check, I'll decide whether to tour it or not.

If my offer is unlikely to get accepted because I'm far from the asking price or it hasn't been on the market long, I won't tour the property. It would waste my and my agent's time with seemingly low odds of success. Instead, I'll submit the offer without touring. If I am persistent, eventually, I will get some stellar deals. Even if they don't initially accept, negotiations may open up that result in an agreement.

If it is likely that the offer will be accepted because I offered close to the asking price or the property has been listed for an extended period of time, I'll schedule a tour before submitting the offer. If you are local, you could attend the tour. Even for properties I'm interested in locally, I ask my agent to tour the property without me. They have more knowledge regarding what issues to look for than I do, so I don't waste my time by attending. However, I have more knowledge regarding which parts of the house can be converted for co-living use. I'll tell them the areas to focus on and have them take measurements to confirm that my remodel plan is feasible. They will send a video of the tour, highlighting the areas of interest, noting the measurements. Sometimes, the listing pictures will look like a space is large enough for a bedroom, or a half bath is large enough to add a shower, but in reality, it is much smaller and won't accommodate my plans.

Assuming you tour or have your agent send a video, return to your analysis and adjust the inputs based on your findings. Perhaps you found that the water heater is old and needs replacing. Work that into your analysis and recalculate your purchase price. Maybe you discovered that you cannot build two additional rooms due to lack of space. Rerun your numbers with your changes in mind. It will likely crush the price you can pay for the property, but that is okay. At the end of this review step of the funnel, the goal is to have the most accurate estimation of the property performance.

Submit Offer

By now you've toured the property or determined that the seller is unlikely to accept your offer. Either way, you have a purchase price that you are confident will produce the performance you need. So, put it in writing!

Even if you feel the seller will not accept, spend the extra time to submit a formal offer. The worst that they could say is no, but they might accept.

Negotiation Tactics

Before sending the offer at the calculated purchase price, confer with your agent about ways to increase the odds of your offer being accepted.

Here are my favorite tactics to deploy.

FLEXIBLE CLOSING AND RENT-BACK

Some sellers are absolute sticklers about price. They'd rather kill the contract than drop the price by even $1,000. If you find yourself negotiating with such a seller, they may be more agreeable if you offer some nonmonetary benefits.

When touring the property, if you notice all the furniture is missing (indicating that the seller has already moved to their new home) they may be interested in a quicker close. If you can close in two weeks rather than the typical thirty days, you could save them thousands in mortgage payments. By default, the residential real estate industry operates on thirty-day closings. However, it isn't that difficult to close in two weeks. Lending is the most likely piece to hinder a two-week closing. However, it is doable if you have all your lending documents organized and your lender is a rock star who works efficiently.

Alternatively, during the tour, if you notice that all of the seller's furniture is still in the house (indicating that they have not moved to their new home yet) offering them an extended closing—perhaps sixty days—could give them much-needed breathing room to take their time finding their next home. Concurrently, you could offer them the option to rent the property back from you after closing until they purchase their next house. Ideally, they will pay you an agreed-upon rent amount during this rent-back period. However in hot markets, renting back to the seller for free can be common.

WAIVE CONTINGENCIES

Contingencies are terms in the contract that allow the buyer to back out and receive any deposits back without penalty. Some common ones include:

- **Inspection contingency:** Allows the buyer to back out based on findings of the property inspection
- **Appraisal contingency:** Allows the buyer to back out if the property appraises below the purchase price
- **Financing contingency:** Allows the buyer to back out if they are not approved for financing

Since these contingencies protect the buyer, not the seller, they weaken the offer. Suppose the seller is presented with two offers, each with identical terms, except one does not have an inspection contingency. In that case, they are likely to choose the latter since there is a lower possibility of the deal falling apart after the inspection.

Ideally, you'd keep all contingencies to maximize your protection. However, as you become experienced and comfortable with your skill set and your team's competency, you may find them less critical and forgo them to make your offer more enticing.

MULTIPLE OFFERS

If the lead is in the likely-to-be-accepted camp, try to submit multiple offers. One offer is at your calculated price, and another at a lower price. For example, the seller may want $500,000, but the calculated purchase price is $480,000. If you offer $480,000 and $450,000, the seller will compare your two offers with less emphasis on their asking price and is more likely to accept one of yours. If you only submit the offer of $480,000, the seller will compare your $480,000 offer to their $500,000 asking price, which may look to them like a steep price cut.

The lower offer must always be sweetened in some way, potentially by offering a flexible closing, rent-back, or waived contingency, as discussed previously.

USE NON-ZERO NUMBERS

Instead of offering exactly $480,000, change the offer so that it does not end in a zero. Randomize the offer a bit, like $481,384. This may seem silly, but it suggests to the seller that you have performed your analysis and calculated the exact offer that works for you. It makes your offer seem nonnegotiable.

FOLLOW UP

Now that you have submitted your offer, the seller may accept it. If they do, great! Move on to the next stage. However, a rejection or counteroffer is to be expected.

If the seller counters your offer, evaluate their proposal, run your numbers, and decide if you can accept it. Submit your counter if their proposal doesn't allow the property to meet your performance criteria. Never purchase a property that doesn't meet your requirements!

You may be stuck in this stage for days, weeks, or even months. Never give up!

If the seller rejects your original offer or your counter, continue to submit that same offer every week. I've often been told "no way," but once the property sits for thirty to ninety more days, sellers are more inclined to accept that offer I've kept at the top of their inbox.

Once you get an accepted offer, move to the next and final stage of the co-living property funnel.

Offer Accepted

Congratulations! After filling the funnel with hundreds of leads, you have a property under contract. But the work doesn't stop here.

Fortunately, paid professionals like your real estate agent, lender, insurance agent, title representative, property inspector, and appraiser will do most of the heavy lifting from here. However, you'll still have some responsibilities, and it is important to be aware of the entire process.

Earnest Money Deposit

First, you will send your earnest money deposit (EMD) to the title company. EMD is a nonrefundable portion of your down payment. If you back out of the deal for a reason not listed as an exception in the contract, or you pass certain deadlines in the contract, then the seller gets to keep the deposit. If you back out for an exception the contract allows, you can get the deposit back. Assuming you close on the deal as planned, the EMD will be credited as part of your funds needed to close.

Title Research

Next, the title company will start researching the property's ownership history and ensure there aren't any owners or liens you are unaware of. Uncovering another owner or lien is rare, but it can happen. This process can take a week or two; you do not need to be directly involved.

Ordering Insurance

You'll need to contact your insurance broker and order your insurance policy shortly after going under contract. There is a deadline in the contract after which you may not receive your EMD back if the insurance options are not reasonable, so you'll want to start this process early. It may take your broker some time to gather your options.

Once they provide you with all your options, you'll select the best one based on premium, deductible, and other policy terms. It is then best to connect your lender and insurance broker, as the lender will need information about the policy you selected.

Inspection

While the title company performs its research, you or your agent will order the inspection. During the inspection, a professional will investigate every part of the house, inside and out, looking for any issues. While most parts of the closing process, like the title research and appraisal, are paid for at the time of closing, the inspection is paid for before the appointment.

It is convenient to have your contractor(s) walk the property during this time and formally prepare a quote if you haven't already. Since co-living remodels are usually pretty simple, I don't get a formal quote until I'm under contract; instead, I rely on my estimate from the earlier stages. However, now that the certainty of purchasing the property is increasing, I want to know if my contractor agrees with my assessment. If the quote exceeds the earlier estimate by a margin large enough that the property performance is altered, you may need to renegotiate with the seller. This is an investment, and the deal has to make sense.

The inspection is also a great time to take preliminary rental listing photos and videos. We'll talk more about how to get the best listing media in Chapter 8: Furnishing, but if you attend the inspection, you can take this time to capture some decent pictures and videos. If you don't attend, you could have your agent do it. As soon as you close on the property, list the existing rooms for rent with the preliminary media you gathered. Yes, the property isn't in its final form yet, as it isn't furnished or fully remodeled, but you can often get lucky and get a few people to sign before all furnishings are there. The quicker you can start making income, the faster you can cover your monthly expenses.

While the contractor(s) are walking the property and your agent is taking photos and videos, the inspector will also be walking the property. Nonfunctioning electrical outlets, burned-out light bulbs, and clogged gutters gutters are a few common issues your inspector may uncover. These are quick and easy fixes. More significant concerns include leaking roofs and compromised foundations. These are much more costly. Regardless of the severity of the issues, once you receive the report from the inspector, you can use it to renegotiate with the seller. You may:

- Not ask the seller to fix an issue, opting to fix it yourself after closing.
- Ask the seller to fix the issue.
- Ask the seller to reduce the purchase price or give you a credit at closing.

Choosing which of these options is best for the deal is part of the negotiation, and a skilled agent can guide you toward the best outcome for the particular deal.

Underwriting and Appraisal

Once you go under contract, your real estate agent will send the purchase contract and any other details to your lender. The lender will begin underwriting the deal, which can take two to four weeks.

You'll likely already be preapproved when the lender reviews your income, debts, and assets and checks your credit. Now that you are under contract, the lender will dive deeper by verifying your income (if required by the loan program) and determining the property's value. To determine the value of the property, the lender orders an appraisal.

An appraisal is a professional opinion of a property's value given by an appraiser. The appraiser visits the property and documents its condition and features. Then, they compare the subject property to similar, or comparable, properties in the area that have recently sold, using their sales prices to determine an appropriate value for the subject property.

Once the lender has collected your personal information, received the appraiser's opinion of value, and reviewed everything, they will approve or deny the loan. If the loan is not approved, you have some options:

- Lower the purchase price to an amount the lender will approve you for
- Bring more money down so that your loan amount is lowered enough to be acceptable to the lender
- Terminate the deal

Final Steps

Once the title company has completed its title research, the inspection has been completed, both parties agree on the resolution to fix any issues, and the lender has approved the loan, you are almost to the finish line! Just a handful of tasks are left to complete before taking possession of the property.

ORDERING FURNISHINGS

Now is the time to purchase your furnishings. We'll further discuss the exact furnishings you need for a co-living property in Chapter 8: Furnishing. While you can wait until after closing, obtaining furnishings early can shave a week or two off your setup process. Be careful with the timing, though.

I made the mistake of ordering everything before the approvals from title, inspection, and lending, assuming everything would be smooth sailing. The closing was delayed by a week, and I spent days going to and from the property, collecting the delivered packages.

If you are confident there won't be delays, I recommend ordering everything a couple of days before closing. In this case, you can get everything delivered straight to the property, so the person setting the property up doesn't have to transport everything there.

If you have concerns about the closing date but still want to order early, you can send everything to your house, or your contractor's, depending on who is doing the setup. Then, the items can be transported to the property after closing.

TRANSFERRING UTILITIES

Before taking possession of the property, you'll want to set up all of its utilities and services, including water, sewer, electric, gas, trash, and internet.

Your agent can tell you which companies supply your water, sewer, electric, and gas. By calling these companies, you can open an account and transfer the utilities from the seller's name to yours.

Depending on the city, there may be multiple trash companies to choose from. When evaluating your options, consider the price and quality of service. Also, ask if they can retrieve your trash cans from the house. One of my trash companies calls this a rollout service. This is a paid add-on that is perfect for co-living properties. Rather than relying on one of your residents to roll the trash cans to the road on trash day, a local trash company can handle it for you.

You'll likely also have multiple options for internet providers. Make the selection based on price, customer service, and speed. Since many people will occupy the house and use the internet simultaneously, you'll want to opt for a fast plan. I'd recommend at least 800 Mbps, especially considering how many residents are students, work from home, or are gamers.

WIRE FUNDS

Your lender will calculate the cash needed to close a day or two before closing. The cash to close is the total amount the title company needs to receive from you: the sum of your down payment, loan costs, title fees, prepaid taxes and insurance, credits, and more.

The title company will require this to be paid with certified funds, either a cashier's check or a wire transfer. A wire transfer is my preferred method, as I can initiate it remotely; however, you may pay with either.

Final Walk Through

On the day before or the day of closing, your agent will do a final walk-through of the property, which you are welcome to attend. This is a final check before you take possession, ensuring that no damages have recently occurred without you knowing, that all the expected appliances are still there, and that the property is as expected.

Closing

The final step is to close on the property! If you are local to the property, you will visit the title company alongside your agent on closing day and sign all of the paperwork with a notary. If you are not local to the property, the title company will send a mobile notary to a place of your choosing.

You can expect to sign more than fifty pages and be there for at least an hour, but you'll officially own the property after all those signatures. Then, your agent will hand you the keys, and you can get to work setting things up.

Example Property

To further describe how to select a property, let's walk through a real example in my portfolio from start to finish.

During a big drive for expansion in my primary market, I found and closed on a property in mid-2024 that was listed on the MLS. It was initially listed in 2023 for $630,000, when the market was heightened. After a few price drops, the property was removed from the market. In 2024, it came back on the market for $530,000—a significant price drop and closer to what it was worth. At this point, it entered my funnel, as it passed my automated filters: in a location I liked, no HOA, single-family home, and greater than 2,050 square feet.

I proceeded to perform some manual checks. I checked Google Street View and saw it was on a corner lot with enough parking for at least ten residents. Since it was in an area with poor access to public transportation, I knew every resident would need their own parking space. Then, I reviewed the listing photos for opportunities to add bedrooms. The property was listed with five bedrooms, but it was 2,600 square feet, leading me to believe that I could add more bedrooms. Fortunately, the seller included pictures of the floor plan in the photos, so getting a game plan together was simple. It would be possible to convert an office into a bedroom by adding a door. A large flex space could be converted into two bedrooms, bringing the total bedroom count to eight. With this information, I moved forward to the analysis.

I input the estimated rents based on eight bedrooms and co-living-specific costs like utilities, cleanings, and shared supplies in a rental property calculator tool. I estimated it would take $15,000 to build the three rooms and fix a few other things, including a 20 percent buffer. I also accounted for three months of mortgage payments as reserves and a $5,000 furnishing budget. As for the loan details, I planned to use a 25 percent down, 8.125 percent interest rate, ten-year, interest-only DSCR loan. I included all other inputs the calculator required that are common for all rentals. Ultimately, the cash-on-cash return at the list price returned 11 percent. My only performance requirement was a cash-on-cash return of 12 percent, so it was a little low. After playing around with the purchase price, I found that getting it for $510,000 would meet my performance requirement.

Since I wasn't too far off the list price, I decided it was worth scheduling a tour. My agent went to the property without me (although it was just an eight-minute drive from my house) and recorded a video walk-through. He focused on areas where I wanted to add rooms, measuring the space and ensuring there would be proper egress. The video confirmed my assumptions.

With confirmation from the video walk-through, I was confident in my calculated offer price. I submitted multiple offers and utilized the non-zero strategy to increase the odds of an offer being accepted. I submitted one offer at $510,244 with a thirty-day close and another at $470,262 with a two-week close. Unfortunately, the seller did not like those offers and said no without countering. No sweat off my back. I was offering on many properties simultaneously, and it was only a matter of time before the funnel produced a great deal. A week later, I submitted the same offer set again. Still no. I continued submitting this offer for two months. Eventually, the property had been listed for over sixty days and still hadn't sold. At this point, the seller was ready to play ball with us. He countered at $520,000, but I stuck to my guns because:

- I knew that at $520,000, my performance requirements weren't met.
- During the tour, I noticed all of their furniture was gone, meaning they were probably in their new house and paying two mortgages.
- The seller had just dropped the price from $530,000 to $525,000, indicating they were eager to sell.

I stuck with the $510,000 offer, and they finally accepted! After eight weeks of offers, we finally went under contract at the price that I needed.

I had thirty days until closing. During the first few days, my lender got the interest rate down 0.5 percent lower than I had expected, so the performance improved. Also, I met my contractor at the property during the inspection to explain my remodel plan. We workshopped the floor plan and devised an arrangement to build the maximum number of bedrooms while still providing the residents with ample floor space. He then wrote a quote that was $1,000 more than I expected but still within my margin of error since I had added a 20 percent buffer to my remodel estimate. During the inspection, I took videos and photos for the initial rental listings, which I then posted on closing day. A few days before closing, once I was highly optimistic that I would close, I ordered all of the furnishings to my handyman's house so he could start the setup process as soon as it closed.

Then, we closed on time, listed the existing rooms, set up the property, started the remodel, and began cash flowing within three months.

Part III

Setting up a Co-Living Property

Chapter 7

Remodeling

Most co-living properties that you purchase will require at least some remodeling. Fortunately, these properties' cash flow is so strong that it is unnecessary to buy total fixer-uppers for a good return, although this can juice the ROI. Usually, you'll be building bedrooms and bathrooms and potentially making some cosmetic improvements.

If your market is prime for co-living, like a college or resort town, you may have purchased a property previously used for co-living. In this case, you may not need to do any remodeling at all, but it is still best to review the current state of the property and make updates or additions to enhance the resident experience and increase your income where appropriate.

Cosmetic and Functional Remodel

While you can buy co-living properties that are in great condition right on the MLS, you may find that the property needs some minor upgrades. Ultimately, residents want a clean house that is updated to match the styles of the last fifteen years and very functional. But you don't need to have super high-end finishes.

To make things look clean and somewhat modern, you'll want to replace any glaring outdated items, like shag carpet, yellowed toilets, and grandma's wallpaper. Additionally, if anything needs repair, like damaged flooring, nonfunctioning appliances, and peeling paint, fix these items so that the property is fully functional for your residents.

Be careful not to go overboard, though, as high-end finishes are more expensive and likely unimportant to your residents. For example, if the kitchen is outdated by a few years, that is probably acceptable unless you are in a highly competitive co-living market. There is no need to replace the countertops with granite or add an elaborate backsplash. Just ensure the kitchen is clean, has recent styling, and has fully functional appliances.

Building Bedrooms

While remodeling, the goal is not to convert every common space into bedrooms to maximize income. Instead, the goal is twofold: to maximize income by building bedrooms and bathrooms and to maintain community space to increase resident satisfaction and the overall resident experience. Sure, having eight bedrooms in a 2,000-square-foot house with no living room seems like it would cash flow on the surface, but providing a great experience to your residents will pay you back many times over by reducing your turnover. Plus, providing such an experience feels good!

I only recommend building the number of bedrooms a property can comfortably support while maintaining at least one living room, the kitchen, a dining area, and a laundry room.

Common locations for adding bedrooms include dining rooms, extra living rooms, family rooms, sitting rooms, offices, flex spaces, basements, and game rooms. An addition, at most, requires building three walls and a closet, adding outlets and ceiling lights, and a door. Depending on the space, it could be as simple as adding a door or closet.

The most creative addition I've done is extending a balcony. I looked at this property listing and found where I could easily add bedrooms, but the performance still wasn't great. After thinking about it for a while, I had an epiphany. On the second floor, a 15'x8' balcony overlooked the entryway. The 8' dimension was too small, so I hadn't considered adding a bedroom there initially. But if I extended that balcony across to the other wall, I could create a massive 200-square-foot room. Plus, the room would be adjacent to the existing primary bathroom. With access to this plumbing, I could even add a private bathroom! That gave the performance boost needed to make this property a viable co-living investment. It worked so well that I bought another property with the same floor plan a few streets over and did the same remodel.

Another creative idea is to turn garage space into bedrooms. I haven't done this, but I imagine it would be more costly, as the garage is less insulated than the house's interior.

Additionally, I've heard of converting the living room into a bedroom and the garage into a huge community space. I have not done this, but I do like this idea, as it adds to your income while still preserving an excellent hangout space. Imagine turning a three-car garage into a community area with a pool table, Ping-Pong table, couches, and work-from-home desks. Residents would love such a space, and the listing photos would look amazing.

When building a bedroom, check city, county, and state regulations for any requirements. Generally, you'll want to verify that you have:

- Met or exceeded the minimum square feet requirement.
- Sufficient space (no single dimension is too small).
- An appropriate number of electrical outlets.
- Sufficient lighting.
- Smoke detectors and carbon monoxide detectors as needed.
- Proper methods of egress.

If your city doesn't have a minimum square-footage requirement, you'll want to set one for yourself. If the city has one, you may want to set your minimum higher to ensure sufficient space for your residents. Residents often store their possessions in their bedrooms, so ample space is essential. I require at least one hundred square feet of floor space, excluding the closet and attached bathrooms. This is the bare minimum, and I prefer larger areas.

In addition to a size requirement, consider a single-dimension requirement. For example, a 10' x 10' room is 100 square feet. A 2' x 50' room is also 100 square feet but isn't quite livable. I prefer not to have a single dimension less than 10', as the room starts to feel cramped, even if it is very long.

Depending on your city's requirements, you may need to have an outlet on every wall or have an outlet every six feet or so.

Lighting in bedrooms is important. A dome light can properly light smaller rooms, but ideally, I like to have multiple recessed lights. Regardless, I always use the brightest LED lights that I can find. Not only does it brighten the room, but in listing photos, it makes the room look newer.

Smoke and carbon monoxide detector regulations vary by city, but they will undoubtedly be required in some capacity. Some areas may require a carbon monoxide detector on each level of the house, while some may require them in each bedroom. Some may require a smoke detector in every room, while some require them within ten feet of each room. Do the research for your market, and be sure to abide by the regulations to ensure the safety of your residents.

You'll almost certainly need to have two ways an occupant can exit the room. The bedroom door is one of them, and the other should provide direct access to the outside of the house. This is typically a window, but it could be an exterior door. The window must meet local egress requirements, such as size and height from the floor. If the room is deep enough underground, you'll need a window well and an egress ladder so that a resident can escape in an emergency.

DIY vs. Professional

If you are early in your investing journey, you might invest most of your cash into purchasing the property with little left for the remodel. In this case, performing the work to build the bedrooms yourself may be enticing, as opposed to paying a contractor, assuming you have the skills necessary.

You can take on parts of the project yourself, especially tasks like framing, sheetrocking, and painting, which often don't require a licensed contractor. However, for electrical and HVAC work like adding outlets, moving light fixtures, and installing vents, you'll probably need to hire a licensed professional as the work is more complex and may require permits and inspections.

For simple room builds you may not need a professional. For example, if you are converting a flex space or office into a bedroom by adding a door, you may not need a contractor. In that case, there are likely already electrical outlets all around the room and the necessary ventilation.

Whether the work is done by you or a licensed professional, check with your local permitting and building department to ensure resident safety and compliance with the law.

Cost and Timeline

As discussed in the Analysis section, the cost to build a bedroom in my market in 2024 is around $3,000 (labor and materials). This will change over time and in different areas. At least half of that cost is attributed to labor, with materials making up the minority of the price.

The project's duration can vary depending on the room and contractor. If you have a single room built, it may take two weeks. But if you have three rooms built next to each other, it won't necessarily take triple the time, as some walls will be shared, and efficiencies will come into play. The price often does not scale linearly for similar reasons. You could estimate two weeks per room, but that should be conservative.

Property Value Impact

You may be thinking, *This is great! I'll add some bedrooms to increase my cash flow and also add value to my property!* This can be the case, but not always. Single-family home property values are determined based on what similar houses sell for nearby. Pricing the home can be tricky if you are the only eight-bedroom property in the neighborhood.

Even if an appraiser could value an eight-bedroom property, are there any families looking to buy homes that large? Probably not many.

When you are remodeling, consider which additions appeal to a buyer and which do not. Remember the house with the balcony extension I mentioned? That house was originally a three-bedroom, so extending that balcony was very valuable. Not only did it add an extra bedroom, bringing the total to a reasonable four bedrooms, but it also added a room with a bathroom. I finished the basement, adding a bedroom, bathroom, and kitchenette, bringing the total bedrooms up to five. That is also very appealing to a buyer. I also converted the dining area and sitting area into bedrooms. Both of these are 10' x 10' and bring the total to seven bedrooms. These are not so appealing. They are small and bring the total bedrooms up to a level with no comparables.

When it is time to sell, I'll look at the surrounding comparables. Are seven-bedrooms selling well? Probably not. Are six-bedrooms selling well? Maybe, but again, probably not. What about five-bedrooms? Probably, since families often want five-bedroom homes. In that case, I'll pay a few thousand dollars to tear those bedrooms down in the future when I sell, and I'll enjoy the extra $20,000 they generate annually in the meantime!

Tearing down rooms when selling is no issue, but what about a refinance? Refinances can prove challenging for co-living properties. If residents already stay there, you cannot just tear the room down before the appraisal. Depending on the bank, a refinance may not require an appraiser to come to the property physically. Instead, the bank may accept a desktop appraisal where they calculate the value virtually, which would be ideal. However, an appraiser will usually visit.

Recently, an appraiser visited one of my properties when I was opening a line of credit. The house had originally five bedrooms, and I added two bedrooms. The appraiser valued it as a five bedroom since there were a lot of comparables, and then gave a $3,000 per bedroom credit for the additional rooms. This worked for me, but I don't think this is common.

Perhaps you can take the doors off some of the rooms and call them flex spaces or offices. If you have active residents in the rooms, they may agree to this for a day. Alternatively, you may need to time a couple of lease end dates to coincide with the refinance so you can remove doors or open a wall for the appraisal. I have not used either of these solutions, but they are ideas I have heard.

Building Bathrooms

After adding bedrooms, you may find that you'll need to build more bathrooms to accommodate everyone comfortably. In most cases, you won't want more than three residents per bathroom. If you have an eight-bedroom house with three bathrooms, one is probably a private bathroom, leaving seven people for the remaining two bathrooms. This results in 3.5 residents to each bathroom, which exceeds the limit. While I have some houses where this is the case, if possible, I'll add another bathroom to accommodate everyone more comfortably.

For co-living properties, bathrooms with showers or bathtubs are the only ones worth counting. You'll often find half bathrooms, which have a toilet and sink. These can be somewhat helpful, as they provide more toilets for the house. The main concern, though, is the number of showers.

On occasion, I have built entirely new bathrooms, but running new plumbing across an existing house can be cost prohibitive. Instead, focus on adding bathrooms near existing plumbing lines if possible. For example, you can often build a bathroom in large laundry rooms and add a stackable washer/dryer if space becomes limited. Alternatively, you could create a new bathroom above, below, or on the other side of the wall from an existing bathroom or the kitchen.

Often, I'll convert half bathrooms by adding a shower stall or bathtub. They are usually too small to house a shower as is, so I have to make them bigger first. This can be done by moving one of the walls into an adjacent room or eliminating a nearby closet and expanding into it. Look for these opportunities and run them by your contractor to see if they are feasible.

DIY vs. Professional

For simple cosmetic upgrades in a bathroom, you can handle much of the work yourself, like installing flooring and mirrors, replacing toilets, and painting the walls.

However, it is best to hire a licensed plumber when running new waterlines or drains as part of building a new bathroom or expanding a half bathroom. These tasks require expertise to ensure proper functionality and compliance with local building codes.

Once again, contact your permitting and building departments to ensure you and your plumber meet the necessary requirements.

Cost and Timeline

Pinning down the cost of any bathroom work can be difficult, as it depends on the existing plumbing. Sometimes, the plumbing will run precisely where you need it to. If not, you'll have to tear up parts of the bathroom and run new lines to tap into the existing lines. The problem is that you may not know the plumbing layout without first opening the floor and walls.

More often than not, the plumbing situation is not ideal, and some extra work has to be done. In this case, converting a half bathroom can cost around $6,000 (labor and materials), but simple conversions can be as little as $3,000. Building a bathroom from scratch will vary, probably in the $6,000–$10,000 range in my market as of 2024.

Property Value Impact

Adding and upgrading bathrooms will always be valuable to a buyer. The buyer will never notice that a closet used to be where the new shower is, and they will not miss it. Similarly, they will not know that thirty square feet are missing from the previously oversized laundry room. Instead, they will be grateful that an extra bathroom is there.

Example Remodel

Below, you'll find before-and-after floor plans of a property in my portfolio. Before you jump to the after images, look at the before pictures and ask yourself how things could best be converted for co-living. This will serve as good practice.

When I purchased the property, it had three bedrooms and two bathrooms on the upper level, with one of those bathrooms being private (not pictured, as I didn't remodel the upper level). On the main level, it had a half bathroom. The lower level had one bedroom and one sort-of bathroom. All in all, it had four bedrooms and three and a half bathrooms. Ultimately, I turned it into eight bedrooms and four bathrooms.

Main Level

In Figure 10, you'll see that the main level originally had two living rooms and a dining room, which were good indicators, as living rooms and dining rooms are often easily convertible. After quick observation, it was apparent that the dining room and one of the living rooms could be converted. Which one of the living rooms, though? I based my decision on the bathroom.

By adding two bedrooms, as seen in Figure 11, I knew another shower or bathtub would need to be added to the house. Since there was a half bathroom, I considered adding a shower to it, before ultimately building a bathroom from scratch. The half bath was pretty small, though, so I dismissed it initially. But then I realized that there was a closet along one of the walls. Removing that closet would add a few extra feet in length, providing enough space for a bathtub/shower combo.

Now that I knew this would become a full bathroom, I returned to the bedroom question. Which living room should be converted? The upgraded bathroom shared a wall with one of the living rooms, so if I could find a way to connect the two, then it could serve as a private bathroom, and the room could be rented for more. So, I added a door to the bathroom, giving the bedroom access, and the existing door remains locked so that everyone in the house does not have access. This only worked because there were two other bathrooms in the house that the other six non-private-bathroom bedrooms could use.

Figure 10. Main level before the remodel

Figure 11. Main level after the remodel

Lower Level

When I purchased the property, the lower level was a mess, as seen in Figure 12. In particular, it was strange that the stairs led straight into the bathroom, which had no door. The only private part of the bathroom was the cramped toilet area surrounded by walls. The shower, however, was out in the open. It had potential, as there was an unfinished storage area and a large third living room.

I knew that the property would become profitable by turning the storage area and the living room into bedrooms, but the storage room was only accessible by passing through the bathroom. After brainstorming with my contractor, we designed a bathroom layout that was private and much more usable, as seen in Figure 13. To allow access to the storage room, we added a door to another wall and removed the existing entry door. This meant I'd need to have a hallway that lessened the floor space of the living room, but it was still well within the bedroom space requirements that I set.

Figure 12. Lower level before the remodel

Figure 13. Lower level after the remodel

The Process
This project was optimistically estimated to take six weeks but took twelve. While this was unanticipated, it ultimately didn't matter a great deal. During the remodel, I listed the existing four bedrooms and started having residents move in. Before they signed a lease, I notified them of the remodel, but no one seemed to mind, as they'd all be at their jobs during the day while the construction was going on.

I prioritized the remodel on the main level, as it would take less time and included a private bathroom, which would rent for more. Once these were built, I rented them and moved on to the basement remodel. As each room in the basement was built, it was listed.

Filling the rooms as they were completed minimized vacancy—much better than having the whole house sit empty for the twelve-week construction period.

Here is a video showcasing the property before, during, and after the remodel: www.BiggerPockets.com/CoLivingBonus.

Usability and Property Value
As we've discussed, parts of a co-living remodel will be useful to a buyer one day, and others will not. So, what is the plan for this property when it comes time to sell?

On the main level, I'll convert the dining room back. Additionally, the door to the living room conversion will be removed to make it accessible to the whole house again. I'll likely leave the two closets for those rooms as they are still useful, and I'll leave the shower in the converted half bathroom. When converting the half bathroom, I had the end in mind when I left the hallway door in place. Future owners can just unlock the bathroom door to be shared by the whole house again. I'll spend a few thousand dollars to undo some of the room conversions, but overall, the property value has increased thanks to the full bathroom.

On the lower level, the living room conversion will be undone, but everything else will benefit the new owner. First, the bathroom actually looks like and functions as a bathroom now since it is walled off with a door. Additionally, the unfinished storage room is much more functional as the bedroom that it is now. Ultimately, adding the bathroom and bedroom will significantly increase the value.

Chapter 8

Furnishing

Furnishing is a crucial part of the co-living setup process. Imagine moving in with random housemates, not knowing who is bringing what. The living room would be a nightmare, with three different couches and two TVs. The kitchen countertop would be littered with multiple toasters and coffee makers. To prevent clutter and confusion, you must provide at least some furnishings for your co-living properties.

If the property was already furnished when you purchased it because it was previously a co-living, mid-term, or short-term rental, then fantastic! Your furnishing workload will be significantly reduced. However, you'll still want to follow the guidance in this chapter to ensure you have every piece of furniture and technology needed to run the best operation possible.

Personally, I don't think you need an interior designer. While they are important for short-term rentals where aesthetics are everything, co-living properties just need to look pretty good and be highly functional—something you can probably design on your own.

To make furnishing easily repeatable, I created a furnishing list with links to all the items I use. It is always up to date with items that balance cost and durability. You can check it out here: www.BiggerPockets.com/CoLivingBonus.

Bedroom Furnishings

The first step when furnishing is deciding whether to furnish the bedrooms. Since it is not a shared space, residents can potentially provide their furnishings, but what is ideal for your property?

Furnished vs. Unfurnished Bedrooms

Determining whether to furnish private spaces can be challenging, as different residents will have their preferences. It is an important choice, though, since you will alienate a portion of the population. If someone has furniture they wish to use in the bedroom but you already have it furnished, they are unlikely to stay with you since they'd have to pay to store it elsewhere. Alternatively, if someone does not have bedroom furnishings and neither do you, they may have to spend cash they didn't account for in their search for new housing.

You could offer both options for a single room; however, the cost and logistics of having someone furnish and unfurnish it, depending on the incoming resident's preference, could prove costly. Instead, you'll need to do your best to determine the preferences of most residents in your market and start with that option. Be open to changing your approach down the road, though, if you find your initial approach ineffective.

If you used the interest form that I recommended in Chapter 5: Selecting a Market when performing your research, you'll notice there was a question asking if the applicant would rather have a furnished or unfurnished bedroom. The response to that question can factor into your decision. If you did not gather such data, you can decide your approach based on the resident type you anticipate attracting.

In my experience, residents who stay for shorter terms are more likely to want a furnished room. They probably don't travel with furniture and won't want to buy any temporarily. Residents who stay longer are likelier to want an unfurnished room, as they'll likely have furniture or be willing to purchase their own since they'll stay for a while.

College students, interns, and traveling workers are among the groups that are more transitory and may want furnished bedrooms. Lower-income workers and young professionals are among the groups that are more permanent and may wish to have unfurnished bedrooms.

Military members may lean either way, depending on the type of military base and assignments available. Some bases have temporary duty (TDY) assignments that last less than six months, so these residents are more likely to want furnished rooms. Alternatively, if the base has many permanent change of station (PCS) assignments, those members will likely provide their own furnishings since they will be there for years.

There are some advantages and disadvantages to each furnishing approach.

If you furnish the bedrooms, your property will experience less wear and tear, as residents won't move their furniture through the hallways, accidentally hit the walls, and damage the paint. However, you will have a higher up-front setup cost and the expense of furniture replacement and repair over time. Also, leaving your property and moving elsewhere is much easier for the resident since they don't have to worry about moving heavy furniture.

If you do not furnish the bedrooms, your start-up costs will be lower, and your residents are likely to stay longer, as moving their furniture is a barrier to leaving. Plus, they decorate their room; thus, it feels more like a home than a temporary place to stay. The main disadvantage is that the walls will become damaged over time as residents move in and out.

Bedroom Furnishings to Provide

If you decide to furnish the bedrooms, be sure to provide the following:

- Bed frame
- Mattress
- Nightstand
- Desk
- Desk chair
- Dresser
- Blinds/curtains
- Decorations
- Bedding

The bed frame and mattress should at least be full size, but if there is enough space, a larger bed would be best to boost demand for a little extra cost. A simple nightstand for setting personal items on one side of the bed will do. Many of your residents will work remotely part time, have their own small business, attend school, or be gamers; thus, they will need a desk for their computer and a nice desk chair. Your room should have a closet for hanging clothes, but the resident will also need a dresser for their folded clothes. Sometimes, when you purchase a house, you'll find that there aren't any blinds or curtains over the windows. I made this oversight when my wife and I bought our first house hack. The house had been recently flipped, but no blinds or curtains were installed. Residents requested blinds or curtains to block the light. Putting up blinds is a simple fix, but ensure you have them. Simple decorations like wall art and fake plants will be appreciated and look great in listing photos. You may want to provide bedding (sheets, pillows, comforter, etc.) and towels, especially if you are listing on Airbnb, as these are assumed amenities. If you are not listing on Airbnb, then bedding may not be required, but having these items in a closet that the resident can access is a good idea. Regardless, when you take your listing photos, be sure to have the bed dressed.

When purchasing these items, focus on balancing cost, durability, and aesthetic appeal. Depending on your target resident, weigh these considerations appropriately. For example, if you plan to list your furnished room on Airbnb, emphasize aesthetics, as listing photos are very important, and competition is fierce.

The furnishings will cost around $1,000 per bedroom in 2024; however, this will surely increase over time.

Shared Area Furnishings

You'll certainly need to furnish the common areas of the house. This includes the living room, kitchen, laundry, and other miscellaneous areas. Below, you'll find some of the most essential items, but consult the extensive furnishing list that I linked.

Living Room

You'll undoubtedly want to provide a couch and a coffee table in the living room. This will allow residents to sit down, relax, and hang out.

Optionally, you can provide a TV. You'll want to mount it or buy a TV stand if you do. Some investors do not offer TVs because they can be a noise source during quiet hours. Personally, I provide a large TV so residents can have movie nights together or watch TV alone during daytime hours, and I have not had any issues. As we'll discuss later, I do have cameras in the common spaces, so if I did have a noise complaint, I'd be able to identify who is causing the issue and contact them to remedy it.

Additionally, you can provide community board games such as Monopoly, Scrabble, and Clue. If you do provide these games, you can encourage game nights as a community event.

Kitchen

I furnish the kitchen like a short-term rental by providing everything residents need to cook besides food and seasonings. Important items include:

- Plates and bowls
- Silverware
- Pots and pans
- Cooking utensils

- Cooking knives
- Strainer
- Drying rack
- Paper towel holder
- Trash can
- Fire extinguisher

As for appliances, I always provide a microwave, stove, oven, refrigerator, toaster, and coffee maker. If the property has a dishwasher installed when you buy it, that's fantastic; however, I wouldn't worry about installing one if it does not. Often, residents just hand-wash their used dishes and put them in the drying rack anyway.

Having the right number of refrigerators in a co-living house is very important, but you probably need less space than you think. In my experience, residents rarely use the fridge because they use DoorDash or another delivery service for most meals. Regardless, I always ensure everyone has their own shelf in the fridge.

The number of shelves determines how many fridges you'll need. If you have eight people, then you'll need a total of eight shelves. Even the most spacious fridges have only six shelves, usually with a freezer drawer on the bottom. Many have only four shelves, with the freezer door on the left and the fridge door on the right. If the property has eight residents and comes with a four-shelf fridge, I'll install another four-shelf fridge. If it already has a six-shelf fridge, I won't buy a four-shelf fridge. Instead, I'll buy a semi-full fridge/freezer combo for the remaining two residents. These are between a mini and a full size, usually around ten cubic feet, and are less than half the cost of a full-size fridge. Depending on the setup, each person will have a door slot or a door slot shared by two people. In the freezer, two people are often assigned to each compartment.

Ideally, the additional fridge(s) can be located within the house: either in the kitchen, if there is space, or in the dining area. It can also go in the garage if you cannot find a spot to keep it inside.

Alternatively, I've heard of operators who will put mini fridges/ freezers in residents' rooms, so this could be an alternative to providing extra fridges in the shared space. I try to avoid this because residents would have to transport their food from their rooms to the kitchen, but if I had no other choice, I would be open to it.

Dining Area

Having a dining area is essential. Since everyone's schedules vary, it is often used for eating alone. Still, multiple residents' schedules will occasionally align, and this space allows them to hang out while eating.

Since it is unlikely to be used by everyone at the same time, there is no need to have a stand-alone dining room. Instead, I'll convert dining rooms into bedrooms if they meet my standards. In this case, I still want to have a dining area, usually near the kitchen, with a decent-sized table and four chairs.

Laundry Room

You must provide a washer and dryer at co-living properties. Residents assume this will be provided and will be very disappointed when they arrive if you don't. When looking at properties to purchase, note if they will come with laundry units. If it doesn't, it isn't a deal-breaker. You'll just need to budget for purchasing them in the analysis.

With so many people in a house, do you need multiple sets of laundry machines? I don't think so. Even in my eight-bedroom properties, I've never received a complaint about a backed-up laundry queue. Unless residents are total procrastinators, they are usually pretty flexible about when to do laundry. If they find that someone else is using the washer, it usually isn't a problem for them to wait to start their laundry.

Bathrooms

It is vital to provide the essentials in the shared and private bathrooms. This includes the shower rod, shower curtain hooks, and shower curtain. The shower curtain does get dingy over time, and usually, residents will just replace it themselves. If someone requests a new one, I will replace it. I also provide bath mats, plunger/brush set, and a small trash can.

Miscellaneous

Whether you furnish the rooms or not, you'll still want to label the bedroom doors with numbers or letters. Also, you will want to install smart locks on the bedroom doors, the front door, and potentially the garage door. I'll go into further detail regarding locks later in the chapter.

Be sure to provide a space for mail and packages to be stored. I'll often find an extra shelf in the laundry room that can serve this purpose, but not always. If not, I'll order a small table to place near the entry where packages and mail can be placed. I'll post a laminated sheet above it indicating that it is the mail area. If there is a key for the mailbox, I'll provide a hanger for it there as well.

Although I have house cleaners, I still provide some items for the residents to use for cleaning, such as a vacuum and a broom. At one property, a resident requested a mop, but by default, I leave the mopping to the cleaners. The vacuum and broom are helpful to the residents when they make a small mess they need to clean up. I'll store these in an empty closet or the laundry room.

You should consider replacing all of the light bulbs in the house. You may not notice it during your first walk-through, but most homes have a variety of different light bulb intensities and colors. I like to use white LED lights throughout the house, as they make everything look new, but even if you decide to use a softer yellow, ensure that they are bright and uniform throughout the house.

Providing decor throughout the house can add to the coziness factor of your property. Consider placing these in the entry, kitchen, living room, and hallways. It doesn't have to be anything fancy, but spending $500 on paintings, fake plants, clocks, etc. makes the property feel like home and drastically increases the effectiveness of your listing photos.

Technology

Equipping your property with the right technology can be a game changer. Today, many products on the market can save investors time at a low cost. New smart products will continue to be released, so always keep an eye out for which products will improve the lives of your residents and ease your management headache.

Internet and Wi-Fi

Providing high-quality internet is a must for co-living properties. Not only is it required for residents who work from home or attend online classes, but it also enables all of the other smart technologies I cover later to work within the property.

The most important factor when choosing between internet companies is speed. I was surprised when I called a few providers for one of my properties and was offered 20 Mbps by one company and over 800 Mbps by the other for the same price! Faster is better; however, I've found that anything over 800 Mbps is acceptable for my residents.

The modem is equally important. Often, the provider can provide you with their modem for a monthly fee. If the modem is reliable, this can be a good route, especially if they will install it and service it for free. Unfortunately, though, I've found that the provided modem can be hit or miss with performance, and connection issues are pretty common. Instead, I now purchase my own modem that is higher caliber than the provider-supplied ones.

The router is the device that distributes the internet wirelessly throughout the house. If you use the provided modem, it likely has a built-in router. However, I've found that these routers don't perform optimally, especially for larger houses, as the signal may not cover the entire house. The best solution is to connect the modem to a mesh Wi-Fi system, which involves installing nodes around the house, increasing the signal's coverage.

Smart Locks

Smart locks are the most essential piece of tech in co-living properties and provide many benefits, including the following:

- Create codes for residents remotely on move-in day rather than physically meeting them
- Easily access the property without needing keys
- Create temporary codes for service providers like cleaners, handymen, plumbers, etc.

I'd recommend installing latching smart locks on all bedroom doors. For the front door and the garage door, you'll install the dead bolt variant. When a resident signs a lease, they'll identify what they want their code to be. Then you can remotely create this pin for the doors they need access to, giving them unique and secure passage throughout the property. I don't install smart locks on the rest of the exterior doors, like side entrances and back porches, as this is just added complexity considering residents enter through the front door 99 percent of the time.

If you decide to rent out garage space, you should install a smart lock on the house's garage door. This way, only residents who are renting garage space have access, reducing the risk of vehicle damage or property theft. If the property has a storage shed, you can rent that out and secure it with a smart padlock.

Most smart locks are battery powered, so you must consider that and create a plan to replace them when needed. I have a repair person walk through all of my properties every quarter. As part of this walk-through, I send them a list of locks that show low battery within the app, and they swap the batteries for me. In the house supply closet, I have batteries stocked for them. However, I've had door lock batteries die unexpectedly, perhaps due to abnormally cold weather or a bad batch of batteries. For this situation, I have an emergency battery box stored at the property.

The locks I use have one or two ways of temporarily booting them up to allow passage. They'll either have 9-volt battery terminals or a USB port on the exterior. In a waterproof box outside the house, I'll provide 9-volt batteries, a USB power block, a twenty-foot USB extension, and a USB-C/micro-USB multi-adapter. This ensures that no matter the type of lock, supplies are always within reach to power the lock temporarily in an emergency. If a resident notifies me that the front door or bedroom lock is dead, I'll direct them to the supplies, have them temporarily power and unlock the door, and then replace the batteries.

Security Cameras

Security cameras are optional but worth considering.

Exterior cameras can be useful for monitoring who enters the property, the condition of the yard, or if someone scrapes a resident's car while it is parked on the street. These can either be doorbell cameras or mounted cameras.

I find interior cameras even more useful specifically for co-living properties. These are not meant to violate privacy and are only placed in shared areas such as the living room and kitchen. They are never placed in private areas, such as bathrooms and bedrooms. They are not continuously monitored. Instead, the footage is stored and reviewed in the event of an incident or complaint regarding another resident.

Although you should have rigorous screening standards that weed out any troublesome residents, it is possible that two residents don't jive well, and a physical altercation breaks out. Simply by having cameras, the chances of such events are significantly reduced, and if they occur, you won't have to rely on personal testimonies. Instead, you can consult the footage and decide how to proceed. Also, most co-living houses are mixed gender. My residents have felt safer with cameras, as it reduces the chance of sexual assault, and if it does happen, I have documentation to prove the offense.

While these are two extreme cases where cameras are helpful, some milder use cases exist. I first installed cameras because I had complaints regarding kitchen cleanliness at one property. Someone was leaving dishes out and eating other people's food from the fridge, but their identity was unknown. As soon as I installed the cameras, both behaviors stopped immediately.

In Chapter 13: Ongoing Management, we'll discuss in depth how to solve conflicts within the house. The best way is to provide hard evidence, and camera footage is some of the hardest evidence you can gather.

If you decide to install cameras, there are many brands to choose from. You can find the cameras I currently recommend in the furnishing list. I've tried battery-operated and wired cameras and recommend the wired cameras. Initially, I purchased battery-operated ones for their ease of installation as I didn't have to worry about proximity to an electrical outlet. Even the most efficient cameras I could find would die within four weeks if placed in high-traffic areas like the kitchen. I now use wired cameras that plug into an electrical outlet. Cable management is more of a hassle, but I don't have to worry about constant battery replacement.

You will likely want to select cameras that can upload footage to the cloud, so you can view it remotely rather than storing it locally.

Research your state and local laws to ensure there are no issues with interior cameras. As you interpret the law, remember that cameras in shared areas are similar to those in apartment lobbies and recreation rooms. If the law is unclear, you can consult an attorney.

Also, check your rental listing platforms' policies, as some may not allow cameras. As of 2024, Airbnb has restricted the use of indoor cameras, so you could face issues if you list there.

Smart Thermostat

Smart thermostats are optional equipment that can further decrease friction between housemates.

I am often acquiring huge houses with two or three levels. The upper and lower levels can have a temperature difference of fifteen degrees between them. If unregulated, the upstairs residents will adjust the thermostat to make themselves more comfortable, and the lower-level residents will change it because the new temperature is unbearable.

In houses this large, the best you can hope for is to make everyone reasonably comfortable. With smart thermostats, you can set the temperature and lock it so that the residents cannot adjust it themselves. Occasionally, I'll get a complaint that it is too hot or cold, and I am willing to make minor adjustments, but not to the discomfort of other residents. Another benefit smart thermostats provide is the ability to detect that the house is empty when they don't sense movement and change the set point to something more economical, reducing your resource usage and utility bills. I only enable this feature if the thermostat is in a good location that can detect traffic, like an entryway or living room.

Most smart thermostats have similar features, but my current recommendation is included in the furnishing list.

How to Furnish

Now that you know what items to purchase, when should you buy them? To get your rooms rented as quickly as possible, I recommend having your online shopping carts prepped a week or so before closing. Once you are a few days away from closing and confident there won't be any delays, go ahead and order everything.

In the past, I have had furnishings shipped to the new property, but $3,000 worth of items were stolen off the front porch because I let them sit for eight hours. Instead, I'd recommend shipping to your personal residence if you are going to furnish the property or to a contractor's property if they are going to furnish it for you.

If you live locally, I don't think setting up the furnishings yourself is a bad idea. It will take you a couple of days to install the locks, put together the furniture, hang the paintings, etc., but once it is set up, you never have to do it again.

If you are remote or don't want to spend the time furnishing it yourself, you can hire someone to do it for you. I hire my contractor to do all of the setups for me. Alternatively, you can hire someone from a service like TaskRabbit or Thumbtack. Provide clear instructions, as they are not interior designers. I record a voice-over using the photos and videos of the property to describe how the doors are labeled, where the extra refrigerator goes, where the living room furnishings go, and more.

As soon as the property is furnished, have it thoroughly cleaned, and then you can have your listing photos and videos taken. We'll talk about best practices for this in Chapter 11: Finding Residents.

Part IV

Managing a
Co-Living Property

Chapter 9

Management Strategy

Co-living is a management-heavy strategy. While I've presented information regarding buying and setting up properties, those are actions performed once per property. On the other hand, property management is hard work that must be endured for the life of the investment. Let's begin by discussing what co-living property management involves and whether you want to do the work yourself or not.

Property Manager Responsibilities

In a co-living property, the property manager wears many hats. Nothing in life comes for free; there is always a trade. The co-living strategy provides an outsized reward at the cost of numerous management responsibilities.

Occupancy and Leasing Management

One responsibility of the property manager is to lease the property and maintain occupancy. This involves listing rooms on various platforms as they become vacant and being available to respond to inquiries as soon as they are received, even outside typical working hours. This requires a flexible working schedule. Immediate replies dramatically increase the odds of snagging the lead before another operator does.

The manager must commit time to reviewing the listing's performance and making adjustments as needed. This is less of a mindless task and more of a critical-thinking task. They must implement new solutions, test them, and iterate to ensure qualified residents continue joining the community. More often than not, this means optimizing pricing and updating the listings to reflect the current rates.

Once the manager has leads flowing in, they should rigorously screen them by reviewing their credit history, performing a background check, calling previous landlords, verifying income, and more.

Once screened and approved, the manager should send the lease to the new resident. A good co-living manager will have a standard lease that they use, but you are welcome to modify it and add terms you deem important. In Chapter 11: Finding Residents and Chapter 10: The Lease, we'll discuss more about how to process applications and create a lease if you are managing the property yourself.

Once a lease is signed, the manager should help coordinate the resident's move-in by setting door codes, sending move-in information, and answering any questions. When someone decides to move out, the manager will coordinate cleaning the bedroom, schedule any needed repairs, and process the return of security deposits.

Resident Experience and Community Building
While leasing is a standard responsibility for all real estate strategies, creating a superb resident experience and building a community is unique to co-living. It serves two purposes. One, it enriches the residents' lives by helping them make friends and bringing more enjoyment to their lives. Two, it reduces property turnover, thus increasing cash flow for the investor.

This responsibility involves planning and facilitating social events that the manager can run in person or remotely.

Creating an outstanding resident experience also involves mediating conflicts among residents. If the right people join the house from the start, conflicts won't be a common occurrence. However they will likely happen at some point, and may require management intervention.

Property Maintenance
The property manager will keep the property in tip-top shape for the owner and residents. The manager can learn about issues requiring maintenance in two ways: reactively, when notified by residents, or proactively, during recurring walk-throughs.

To be notified by residents, the manager must be available 24/7 to take emergency calls. This doesn't mean they always need to be awake, but their phone should always be within reach so that they can address emergencies immediately. Nonemergencies should come during regular hours and are less pressing but still essential to address in a timely manner.

While the manager does not have to perform the walk-throughs physically, they must schedule someone to do them. We'll talk about this more in Chapter 13: Ongoing Management.

Once issues are identified, the property manager is responsible for selecting the appropriate service provider and scheduling the repair or replacement.

Financial Management and Reporting

The property manager has limited financial responsibility. They are not the bookkeeper, as they do not keep track of all property expenses for you. However, they collect room rent and may pay for some expenses like repairs and maintenance. You, as the owner, are still responsible for making the mortgage payments, utility payments, and anything else not covered by the property manager.

The property manager will issue payments to you monthly and send a report detailing all of the recent income and expenses.

Property Manager Options

Now that you are aware of co-living property-management responsibilities, you need to decide whether you have the time, energy, and skill set to fulfill this role or if you should pay someone else to do it for you.

Self-Management

The first option is to manage the property yourself. Unless you work a high-stress job with minimal hours to spare in the week, I'd recommend starting here, even if you have the money to pay for a manager. There is a stark difference between co-living and traditional management, and it won't be easy to oversee the manager without knowing the ropes.

If you are a house hacker like I was when I started, you'll undoubtedly be self-managing. While living in the property with your residents, put forth the time and effort to try new management techniques, gather feedback from your roommates, and iterate. There is no better way to build your systems and strategies than while living with your housemates. You can learn from experts Amelia McGee and Grace Gudenkauf as they breakdown the self-managing world in their book, *The Self-Managing Landlord: More Profit, Time, and Peace of Mind with DIY Rental Property Management* (www.BiggerPockets.com/ ReadSelfManagingLandlord).

Regardless of whether you are house hacking or not, self-managing costs $0! The actual cost is your time. When you purchase your first property, you'll spend more time on every task, since you'll be learning. The tasks will be completed more efficiently as you gain experience. When I bring a new property online with eight vacancies to fill, I probably spend five to ten hours per week listing the units, renewing the listings, adjusting the pricing, replying to inquiries, and processing applications. Once I have successfully filled all vacancies, my workload consists of handling maintenance requests, replenishing the shared supplies, and performing miscellaneous tasks, all of which require approximately two hours of my time per week.

Beyond the workload, no one cares as much about your investment as you do, so the quality of the experience for your residents will likely be the highest for this option. By self-managing as taught in this book, your residents will feel that you care for them and want to make a meaningful difference in their financial and social situation.

Third-Party Management

If you do not have time to self-manage your co-living property and you have the funds to do so, hiring third-party management is an option. A third-party manager is a business that professionally manages properties. Managers who handle rooms charge around 15 percent of the gross rent—much higher than the 8–12 percent that traditional property managers charge.

If you hire a third-party manager, know what you are paying for. There are online businesses that many refer to as "management companies," but they are not full-service and instead primarily advertise your rooms and handle rent collection. They are less involved in day-to-day management activities than traditional managers.

Third-party managers can be challenging to find. Most traditional property-management companies will not accept room rentals due to their inexperience. Even if you search the web for "Room Rental Management <city>," you are unlikely to find results. You'll need referrals. If you are already operating in the market, then you probably know someone who is familiar with a room-management company, so make use of your connections. Otherwise, search local Facebook groups and BiggerPockets forums for posts related to room management. Post to Facebook groups and BiggerPockets forums if you still come up empty-handed.

In-House Management

The next level up from self-management, and what I think is the best solution, is to hire an in-house manager. I don't mean having your manager live in the house; rather, I mean hiring and training someone yourself instead of hiring an outside company specializing in property management.

Unlike hiring a third-party property manager, there will be a significant up-front time investment.

You'll have to attract applicants and interview them to make a selection. Once you decide who your property manager will be, you'll need to train them to use all of your systems and follow all of your processes. Finally, you'll have to periodically evaluate their work and provide feedback.

Once you've done the up-front work, you should have significantly less involvement.

It is unlikely that you will hire someone who has already managed rooms before, so you'll have to self-manage to gain experience before hiring and training a manager. With this strategy, you will have to hand over some cash, although much less than required for a third-party manager. Virtual assistants are often ideal choices as hires, as all co-living management can be performed remotely from another country, and they cost far less than U.S.-based employees (usually $6–$15 an hour). For example, I pay my virtual assistants around $10 an hour. My virtual assistant who focuses on property management spends about twenty hours a week for a total of about $800 per month. That is only around 3 percent of my gross rent versus the 15 percent that a third-party property manager costs!

Can you hire an in-house manager when you only have one property? Probably not. Most virtual assistants will want to work full time, but some will be willing to work part time. I decided to hire my first manager when I had three properties (housing nineteen residents). These properties were mostly stabilized and took six hours or less per week to manage. This workload was not enough for most virtual assistants. However, I had other responsibilities I needed help with, as I was rapidly expanding. I needed assistance finding and analyzing properties and coordinating the furnishing and remodeling. This increased their workload to twenty hours a week. I'd say once you have twenty hours a week of work, you can probably start to hire, although your hiring pool will be more limited than if you had forty hours per week of work.

Where can you find virtual assistants? You can either source your leads from a virtual assistant agency or find them on your own.

If you have some capital you are willing to spend and are looking to save time, hiring from a virtual assistant agency is the way to go. The agency will deliver prescreened applicants who are ready for interviews. Some agencies will charge a one-time fee for this service, and others will charge an ongoing fee. They may even offer additional services, such as helping you document processes and manage payroll.

Otherwise, you can make job listings yourself and put them on various listing platforms. As the inquiries roll in, you can have them fill out a Google Form that helps you narrow the pool down. Then, you can schedule interviews with the most qualified candidates and make your hire. Some of the best options for listing that I've found are Upwork, Fiverr, Indeed, LinkedIn, and Onlinejobs.ph.

Chapter 10

The Lease

Before renting your newly acquired property, you'll need a legal agreement between you and the future resident to define how and when rent is paid and the responsibilities of each party. This will usually be a lease, although other methods, such as membership agreements, are becoming more popular. I'll discuss leases exclusively; however, similar principles could apply to membership agreements.

You can draft the initial version of the lease yourself or have a lawyer draft it for you. Regardless, a lawyer should always review the final version to ensure it is legally binding.

Standard Lease Terms

Many aspects of a co-living lease will be similar to one for a traditional rental, as the basic idea is the same: Someone is paying you to provide them with housing. Let's start with the terms included in any lease agreement. This is not an exhaustive list; these are just some of the most important terms explained.

Length and Type

First, you'll want to specify the start and end date of the lease. The length may vary depending on your target resident type. If you rent to longer-term residents (low-income workers, young professionals, etc.), you may have a six-month or one-year duration. If you rent to shorter-term residents (students, interns, traveling workers, etc.), you may opt for one to three months.

You will then define what happens when the lease term ends: fixed end or month-to-month.

FIXED LEASE END

A fixed lease end means that the lease ends on the decided end date. Residents must sign an extension or a new lease if they wish to stay longer.

This can be a great option to avoid seasons in which it may be harder to re-rent the unit. For example, if a resident signs a six-month lease in January, it will end in June. Generally, most markets have the highest rental demand in the summer, so filling this unit shouldn't be an issue. However, if they decide to extend in June, a six-month extension would cause a vacancy in January, a potentially difficult time to find a new occupant. Instead, you can be strategic about the extension and have it end at a more ideal time, perhaps in April or September.

If you choose to, you can offer a slight discount on rent if they agree to sign a longer extension because this lowers your risk of near-term vacancy. If you have an $800-per-month room that takes three weeks to fill, that is a loss of $600 for the time it sits vacant. By offering a twelve-month lease for $790 per month, you are forfeiting $120 each year, but you are kicking that $600 loss down the road.

If you decide to use the fixed lease end, be sure to speak with your residents about their options at least three months before the lease expires. If they do not sign an extension by two months before the end of the lease, start advertising it for a new resident to reduce the time it sits vacant as much as possible.

MONTH-TO-MONTH

Another option is to have the lease become month-to-month at the lease end date. This means that the resident may have a six-month initial lease length, and once that is reached, the lease automatically renews on a monthly basis. This is less of a paperwork headache, as you won't have to send out extensions, but it does mean you may get stuck with a difficult vacancy in the dead of winter if someone decides to move out then.

Month-to-month options are appealing to co-living residents, as they provide more flexibility after the initial term. You may get a slight increase in demand, but the resident can leave on a whim, increasing your turnover. This type of lease can be beneficial for the investor, as you can more readily make adjustments to the rent (usually with a thirty-day notice) rather than waiting until the end of the lease and adjusting as part of the extension.

If you choose the month-to-month option, include a clause stating that they must provide you with a thirty- or sixty-day notice before moving out. Once they give this notice, you can start advertising the room to line up the following occupancy.

Rent and Security Deposit

You'll also want to state the rent amount, any utility fees, and the due date. I recommend having rent due on the first of each month to keep things simple. If you allow room rents to be due at different times, it can become complicated as your portfolio grows.

Also, you'll want to define how the rent is paid. I'd advise against accepting cash, as this could be a huge hassle. Instead, I require that rent be paid through my online rental portal. Checks and cash are not accepted. You may consider accepting payments through Venmo or Zelle with your first property since most residents will use those services. This can work, but especially as you scale, I'd recommend using property management software to collect rent, as it is much more organized and will reduce the chance of a missed payment going unnoticed. We'll discuss property management software in Chapter 14: Tools.

Late fees should also be defined in the lease. Many states have regulations surrounding late fees, so research the topic or ask a lawyer. Is it a flat $50? Is it $10 per day? Is it 5 percent of the rent amount? Also, you'll want to specify when the late fee occurs. Is it charged after one late day or one late week?

Lastly, if you choose to have a security deposit, be sure to define its amount and the circumstances in which you can keep portions, likely for damages to the room or property and unpaid rent.

Depending on your state and local laws, you may be required to keep security deposits separate from the rent or in a trust account. Additionally, you may be required to pay any interest accrued while holding the deposit to the resident when they leave. So, be sure to research the laws for your specific situation.

Breach of Contract

You'll want to detail what happens if the resident violates the lease. Lease violations are commonly caused by failing to pay rent, damaging the property, or not following the rules and regulations.

The steps to take in case of a lease violation vary by state. Typically, you'll have to send a notice describing the violation, giving them time to cure the issue. You can begin the eviction process if they fail to cure.

Evictions can be very messy and expensive so I try to avoid them at all costs. First, I usually explain the problem and ask if they would agree to terminate their lease early without penalty, and they often agree to this. If they don't, eviction proceedings will follow. This option is not listed in the lease, but you may consider it before filing for an eviction.

Occasionally, I get requests from residents to leave before the end of their lease. There are a few options, so you should consider them and include one or more of them in the lease. That way, the solution is clean when you receive this request.

First, you can charge an early exit fee in exchange for them ending the lease prematurely. You may choose the fee amount as long as it is in line with local law, but it is usually one to two months of rent. This is the route I prefer as it is very straightforward and appropriately compensates me for the time spent looking for a replacement and the money lost while the room is vacant.

Alternatively, you can replace the outgoing tenant with a new one. This is the option that residents sometimes request. They'll ask if they can continue paying rent until I find a replacement. I typically shoot this down because it is not in my best interest. If there is another vacant room in my portfolio, I'd much rather assign a qualified applicant to that one instead of replacing the resident who wants to leave early. As an exception, I'll allow the outgoing resident to present me with an applicant as a potential replacement. As long as they meet my screening criteria like everyone else, I will accept them and allow the original resident to move out early.

If either option does not work, you can legally hold them accountable for the contract end date and require that they keep paying as agreed. If possible, I try to implement one of the previous solutions, though, because I don't want someone in the community who doesn't want to be there. That can sour the vibe of the entire house. But this is a business, and it can be worth having them finish their lease to collect the promised rent.

Co-Living Specific Terms

While everything we've discussed so far is common and found in a typical lease, regardless of strategy, there are some terms specific to co-living that you'll want to ensure are included.

Animals

Allowing or disallowing animals is a touchy subject, especially with co-living rentals. A decent portion of your applicants will have animals, so having a restrictive policy will exclude them, causing it to take longer to fill your property. On the other hand, since co-living properties have lots of shared areas, allowing animals can discourage applicants who do not wish to live with animals. No matter your choice, you will alienate a portion of the rental pool.

PETS

Allowing pets does invite some risk. First, there is some risk of the animal attacking a resident or another resident's pet. To reduce this risk and your liability, you may want to allow only specific sizes or breeds of animals. Second, with so much of the population having allergies to certain animals, there is a high likelihood that a current or future resident will have allergies to an incoming pet. You could survey the current residents to see if they would be okay with someone bringing a pet, but you never know what allergies a future resident might have. So, if your policies do allow pets, be sure to notify all future applicants that there are currently or may in the future be pets in the property. Lastly, there is a risk of noise complaints, specifically with dogs. If not properly trained, dogs may bark at passing cars, other residents, or noises like doorbells. This could lead to noise complaints from other residents and a poor household vibe.

To balance risk and alienate as little of the rental pool as possible, I've chosen not to allow pets, like dogs and cats, that must pass through shared spaces. However, I will allow pets caged in a resident's room, like hamsters, reptiles, and fish, that will not make noise or pass through common areas, inducing allergic reactions.

EMOTIONAL SUPPORT AND SERVICE ANIMALS

Emotional support animals (ESA) differ from pets in that they provide therapeutic benefits to those with emotional disabilities. An ESA does not need training but does need to be documented by a licensed mental health professional. Service animals are specifically dogs—or miniature horses, oddly enough—that are trained to assist those with disabilities and require training. Applicants with these types of animals have protections under the Federal Housing Administration and the Americans with Disabilities Act.

For ESAs and service animals you cannot charge pet fees or deposits and often cannot deny an applicant, even if you have a no-pet policy. In rare cases, such as in shared co-living properties, there may be justification for denying someone with an ESA or service animal if allowing them would "fundamentally alter the nature of [the] service, program, or activity."[7] This determination should be made on a case-by-case basis and supported by clear, specific evidence. Potential reasons allowing an ESA or service animal may alter your business include:

- Animals in shared living situations may interfere with the community because of noise and cleanliness.
- Other residents, or future residents, may have allergic reactions to animals.
- The presence of animals may increase your vacancy, impacting your income, as some applicants may not want to live with animals.

Consult with an attorney to ensure you comply with federal, state, and local laws when considering a denial based on this exception.

Rules and Regulations
The general portion of the lease is probably written in lawyer jargon, but for the Rules and Regulations section, I like to provide a bulleted list in plain English terms to prevent confusion or misinterpretation from residents.

COMMUNITY RESPECT
The idea behind community respect is to relay the expectation that everyone should be kind, items should not be stolen, and noise should be kept to a respectful level. Here are some example rules:

- Engage with fellow residents in a friendly and considerate manner.
- Other residents' personal items should not be used or taken without permission.
- Items provided by the property, such as furniture, kitchen appliances, and cookware, should not be taken from the property.
- Quiet hours are from 10 p.m. to 9 a.m. During these hours, no noise should be heard outside of your bedroom.
- Excessive noise outside of quiet hours is not permitted.

---

[7]   "Reasonable Accommodations and Modifications," U.S. Department of Housing and Urban Development, accessed January 15, 2025, https://www.hud.gov/program_offices/fair_housing_equal_opp/reasonable_accommodations_and_modifications.

PROPERTY CARE

The property care section describes how all shared areas should be kept clean and clear of personal items. Early on in my co-living experience, I allowed residents to bring their own living room furniture, and I ended up with three couches and two TVs in one living room. Instead, it is preferred that the residents use what is provided so as to not infringe on the other residents' use of the shared spaces.

Residents must pay for any damage that they cause. When they move out, any damage to their room will obviously be their fault, but proving who caused the damage in the shared areas can be more difficult. If you have cameras, that may help, but expect to use some of your cash flow to pay for damages in common areas. I want residents to hang pictures or art and make it feel like home, but I only allow doing so with 3M Command Strips or something similar that will enable them to hang items without driving nails into the wall. This allows for room turnovers with a quick clean rather than involving a repair person every time to patch holes. Here are some example rules to clear up ambiguities on who caused what damage to shared areas:

- Keep shared spaces free of personal belongings, including furniture and decor.
- Ensure that your room and shared areas are kept clean and well maintained.
- Take responsibility for any damage caused by you; you will be held accountable for associated repair costs.
- Only 3M Command Strips may be used to hang items on walls; nails, tacks, and other methods are prohibited.

GUEST GUIDELINES

You'll want to establish policies regarding guests. I prefer to allow guests to stay six nights per month. If someone has a significant other, this policy allows them to stay over on occasion, but feel free to customize this policy to your liking.

Additionally, it is important to state that the guest must also follow all house rules and that any violation of the rules is the resident's fault.

Here are some example rules:

- Guests are permitted to stay up to six nights per calendar month. If more than one guest stays overnight, each guest counts as a separate night (e.g., two guests staying one night counts as two overnight stays).

- All guests must adhere to house rules and regulations. The hosting resident is responsible for their guests' actions and compliance with all community standards.

HEALTH AND SAFETY

Health and safety are paramount in co-living properties and are achievable if residents follow specific rules that promote a healthy environment. In this section, you'll want to discuss your smoking and pet policies.

You will need to specify how many people can occupy a room. I exclusively allow one resident per room, but other operators have successfully rented to couples.

Lastly, if you have security cameras, disclose them and relay the benefits.

Here are some example rules:

- Smoking is not allowed inside or on the property.
- No animals are allowed except caged, quiet pets that always remain in your room (like fish or reptiles). Pets must not enter or pass through common areas so as to maintain allergen-free shared spaces.
- Each room has a maximum occupancy limit (one person per room unless otherwise specified).
- Common areas and exterior spaces may have 24/7 security cameras to help maintain the property's condition and promote a safer living environment. These cameras can assist in quickly resolving any disputes or concerns. Cameras are never placed in private areas, such as bedrooms and bathrooms, ensuring your privacy is respected. While not actively monitored, the footage provides peace of mind and is referenced only if an incident occurs.

Addenda

If you offer additional services like a garage or storage space for an extra fee, you could include those in the lease agreement. Instead, I've found it is easier to use an addendum.

An addendum is a document that supplements the lease and adds clauses without changing the existing terms of the agreement. Addenda could be agreed to upon lease signing or any time afterward.

It is common for residents to be living at the house for months before they decide to rent a garage space. In this case, using an addendum is much easier than drafting an entirely new lease. In this particular addendum, I define how much of the garage is available for their use (usually one bay), what it is used for, how much it costs, and when the payments are due.

As for its use, I specify that the garage bay is only for storage and parking. Also, renting a garage bay grants them access to park in the driveway in front of the bay, so if they'd like, they can store things in the garage and park in front of it. The storage agreement is similar.

Chapter 11

Finding Residents

Now let's chat about filling your property with residents. It's easy to fill your property with just anybody, but finding the right people is imperative to running a shared house with good vibes and minimal issues.

You'll find that this chapter is structured very similarly to Chapter 6: Selecting a Property. Whether you have a single co-living property or one hundred, you'll have a much higher volume of applicants come across your desk compared to a traditional single-family property where you must find a new family every few years. Keeping co-living properties occupied is a year-round commitment. Even if your average resident stays for twelve months in an eight-bedroom property, you can still encounter a move-out every forty-five days. At this frequency, it is paramount that you have an efficient process for systematically listing vacancies, screening applicants, and getting leases signed.

Screening Criteria

The first step is to establish your screening criteria, similar to the performance requirements you set when looking for a property. You must be aware of Fair Housing laws to avoid legal issues due to discrimination. Read Heather and Brandon Turner's *The Book on Managing Rental Properties* (www.BiggerPockets.com/ReadManaging Rentals) for a thorough breakdown of these requirements.

While there are many requirements that you could have, we'll discuss the ones that I think are most important for co-living properties, but feel free to add your own.

Income

An income requirement is essential to ensure the applicant can afford the rent and pay it on time. It is common for landlords to require the applicant's income meet at least three times the monthly rent, but I've chosen to set mine to two times to allow lower-income applicants to qualify.

While you should have a similar requirement, very few co-living applicants will fail this criteria. As long as they are receiving at least minimum wage, they can usually pass if they are full-time employees.

The instance where I've seen applicants fail is when they only work part time. Check your local regulations, as some areas have restrictions against income requirements.

Credit Score

Credit score requirements are standard for traditional long-term rentals but not necessarily for co-living properties. A higher credit score indicates that an applicant has a history of paying their debts on time, so having a requirement does help you get higher-quality residents. However, some resident groups are prone to having lower credit, and thus, it may take you a very long time to find a qualified applicant if your requirements are strict. For this reason, I know co-living investors who forgo the credit score requirement, especially when they rent to lower-income or student groups.

I have a credit score requirement, which is relatively low at 550. Credit Karma defines this as poor credit. Many of my residents fall in the 550–600 range, but the rent is so low that I rarely see a missed payment. Ultimately, it is standard practice not to have a requirement or to have a low one in the co-living space.

Occupancy

You can also screen based on the number of occupants an applicant will have in their room. Effectively, limiting a room to one occupant prevents couples or single parents with children from moving into the home. While I would love to serve these groups, the other residents in the house are under the assumption that there will not be children or couples, as it would mess with the household dynamic.

For this reason, I only allow one occupant in each room, but other co-living investors sometimes allow two occupants to move into larger rooms. You can charge a premium for allowing two occupants to a room (typically 20–50 percent more than the base price), and they tend to stay longer than a single occupant, as it is difficult for them to find another room that accommodates couples.

Pets

Depending on your preference for allowing or disallowing pets in the property, you'll want to define that as part of your screening criteria. Revisit Chapter 10: The Lease, where I describe both options in detail to help you decide.

Criminal History
Investigating criminal history is crucial for properties with shared spaces. When I receive a background report, I usually do not see criminal history—especially considering that most applicants are very young. If I see any history, it is usually just speeding or parking tickets. Of course, accepting someone who forgot to add meter time poses little risk to your other residents. However, I do not approve applicants with theft, violence, or felony-level crimes. The other residents in the house are entitled to a safe living environment, and I am responsible for creating it. By screening out anyone who has committed theft or acts of violence in the past, you will significantly reduce the risk of major issues in the household.

Eviction History
You can screen applicants based on eviction history. Most applicants are young and have not experienced an eviction, but I'll see history of evictions occasionally.

An eviction could have been filed due to nonpayment of rent or lease violations. Since many applicants have low income and are trying to get back on their feet, you may choose to accept those who have had nonpayment issues if they have made a substantial change in their life, but be wary of lease violations. If these were recent lease violations, they may behave similarly at your property and cause issues in a shared housing environment.

Smoking
You have the ability to disallow smokers. While smokers are less common than they used to be, especially among younger applicants, you will still come across some. As secondhand smoke causes health issues to other residents and the smell can seep into the walls, flooring, and furniture, I do not allow smokers at all. It is too great of a risk, especially since there is a large pool of applicants who do not smoke.

Listing Photos and Videos
Before you start the process of creating your advertisement and screening applicants, you'll want to have your photos and videos prepared. You probably took some preliminary photos and videos during the inspection, but going forward, you'll want updated media of the recently cleaned property with all its furnishings.

I don't think hiring a professional photographer and videographer for co-living properties is necessary. This is essential for short-term rentals, but your room-rental competitors often have unprofessional, crooked photos with all the lights off. Using a decent cell phone camera, opening all the windows, turning on the lights, and editing a little will be sufficient for your co-living listings. You may hire a photographer, especially if you are remote, but don't feel obligated to.

For the photos, capture every interior area (living room, kitchen, laundry room, bathrooms, and bedrooms) and the front and backyard. You may want to edit to correct any crookedness and brighten the environment.

For the videos, you can shoot the entire property in one take or record in segments. If you record in segments, you can piece together unique videos for each listing that share all of the common space footage with a video of the individual bedroom tagged on. If you record the whole house in one take, you can just have a single video showing all rooms and common spaces. I opt to make a unique video for each room so that applicants don't have to waste time watching parts of the video to find the room they are interested in, but this does add editing time.

You can consider talking throughout the videos as if you are giving the tour in person. Sell them on the community's benefits, how the lease works, where payments are made, etc. If you have a videographer take the videos for you, then you can just record a voice-over later if you choose.

I upload my tours to YouTube and provide links when someone shows interest.

The Resident Funnel

Similar to selecting a property, you can find qualified residents using a funnel. The co-living resident funnel, seen in Figure 14, provides a system for systematically processing all leads in a fair, uniform, and efficient manner.

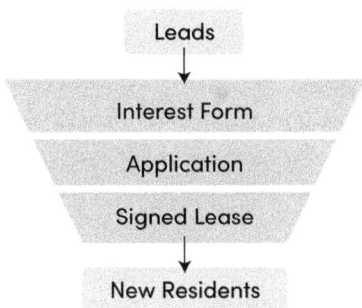

Figure 14. The co-living resident funnel

Leads

You need to put leads into the funnel. I'll discuss two approaches: on market and off market. Like properties, you can advertise your rooms in marketplaces that applicants search (on market) or you can seek out the applicants directly (off market). Then, we'll discuss what should be included in your advertisement and how to best price your rooms.

ON-MARKET LEADS

The most obvious and easiest way to find residents is to list rooms on websites created solely for connecting applicants with landlords. I see most of my applications come through these channels.

I'll provide the sites I've had the most luck with, but the best sites can vary between markets. Test the services I mention, but also search the web for "<city> roommates." When someone looks for a room in your city, this is exactly what they will search for. Being listed on the top-resulting websites is a must.

Once you are listed on all the platforms, monitor how many messages you are getting from each. You may decide to drop the lowest-performing platform to save time and potentially money (some services are paid).

Ensure that you are at the top of the search results for all of these sites as often as possible. If they have a "renew listing" feature, renew the listings at least every week. Some sites do not have this option, so you may want to periodically delete and repost your listings to bring them to the top of the search results.

Facebook Marketplace

Facebook Marketplace is a hot spot for room listings in all markets nationwide. I find that a majority of my traffic comes from here. You'll need to create a Facebook account if you don't already have one. Once you've created an account, Facebook often doesn't allow you to post immediately on Marketplace, as they have a waiting period for new users. If you already have a Facebook account, you should be ready to post.

When creating your listing, select the "private room in a shared property" option. When applicants search the platform, they'll most likely select the "room" filter option, allowing your rooms to appear in the results. As of the writing of this book, Facebook doesn't allow multiple rooms to be listed at the same address. You cannot have separate listings for each room in a property. Instead, you'll have to create one listing and just describe the pricing and features of each room in the description.

Facebook Marketplace is free to list, though you can optionally pay to boost your listing to receive more traffic.

Roomies

While Facebook Marketplace allows you to list personal items, traditional long-term rentals, rooms for rent, and more, Roomies is explicitly built for room rentals. This is great, as it offers some advantages that Facebook Marketplace does not, such as allowing multiple room listings per house, a section to describe the other roommates, and categories for furnished, unfurnished, private bathroom, and shared bathroom.

Roomies is free to list if you have ten active rooms or less. You will have to upgrade the account if your number of active rooms exceeds this limit. To increase visibility and possibly interest, you can pay to push your room to the top of the search results.

Roomster

Roomster is built for room rentals and has room-specific features similar to Roomies.

Applicants can browse Roomster for free, and landlords can list their properties for free. However, to reply to messages, the landlord and applicant must both have paid accounts. For this reason, I've had less traffic on Roomster than other sites, but it might still be worth temporarily upgrading to the paid version of the site to gauge interest in your market.

Zillow

Zillow is not only useful when searching for potential properties to purchase; you are also able to advertise your rental properties. Select the "room for rent with a shared living space" option when listing. Since Zillow is one of the most popular rental listing platforms across all rental types, it makes up a large portion of my room rental inquiries.

Zillow is free to list on, and you can have multiple room listings for a single address simultaneously.

Airbnb

All previous listing sites will support furnished and unfurnished rooms. If your rooms are furnished, then you will want to become familiar with listing on Airbnb. If they are unfurnished, you'll be unable to list them here. While this book focuses on renting rooms monthly or longer, you can rent your rooms out for days on Airbnb. However, I'll concentrate on longer-term tenancies with a minimum stay of thirty days or longer.

Airbnb works much differently than other platforms, as it handles some legal and financial aspects of renting.

A lease is not required on Airbnb, as the platform has built-in agreements for both parties. I recommend having the resident sign a lease of your own, in addition to Airbnb's agreements, so that you have more protection. Once you've accepted a guest, you can access their phone number and email to send an electronic lease. If you do this, mention in your description that you'll require a lease to be signed before move-in.

Unlike other platforms, Airbnb facilitates payments from residents. They will skim about 14 percent off the top for their services. If you can fill your vacancies more quickly by adding Airbnb to the mix, this can be worth the cost.

Airbnb is driven by reviews. While you should be a great landlord no matter what, you must put in extra effort while advertising on Airbnb, as a bad review can damage your ability to rent on the platform in the future.

Furnished Finder

If you decide to furnish your rooms, Furnished Finder can be a good service to garner interest. The platform is built for rentals with a thirty-day minimum stay, and for renting entire furnished houses as well as furnished rooms.

Furnished Finder works a little differently than most listing platforms. Once you list your rooms, applicants often won't directly reach out to you. Instead, Furnished Finder will notify you when someone has created an account and is searching for housing in your area. You'll then need to take the initiative and reach out to them. Unlike Airbnb, you'll handle the leasing and rent collection yourself.

Furnished Finder does require the landlord to have a paid account, but applicants can search and use the platform for free.

PadSplit

PadSplit is another listing service, available in specific markets, that you can use to advertise your rooms. To list on PadSplit, each bedroom must be furnished, and you commit to renting all rooms exclusively through their platform, meaning you cannot advertise elsewhere or manage residents outside the platform.

Like Airbnb, PadSplit handles rent collection and agreements for residents' stays. However, while Airbnb collects rent monthly for more extended stays, PadSplit collects rent weekly. Additionally, PadSplit uses membership agreements instead of traditional leases to define the terms of the resident's stay.

Beyond advertising, PadSplit has software features that help you manage the residents once accepted, such as room pricing suggestions and resident communication.

PadSplit charges landlords a percentage of the collected rent in exchange for its services. After paying the application fee, potential residents can request housing from the available hosts on the platform.

OFF-MARKET LEADS

In addition to listing your rooms on websites and waiting for applicants to contact you, you can proactively reach out and find the applicants. While this does require more work, you'll have much less competition if you reach the applicant before they become interested in someone else's listing.

Start by brainstorming all the places your target resident visits often. Are they military? If so, you can try posting flyers on base and networking with the housing office. Are they teachers? If so, post flyers in the school break room and network with the hiring representatives. Are they students? If so, post flyer advertisements all over campus. I'll contact my residents and give them flyers to post for me, if they are willing. If they bring in a lead who signs a lease, I'll reward them with a discount on their next rent payment. Win-win!

Let everyone in your network know you are always looking for residents. At least once per month, I'll receive a text from a friend or colleague who knows someone moving to town who wants to save on rent.

You can regularly remind your current residents that you are seeking new applicants. I send a mass email once per month to all who currently stay with me, reminding them that if any referral they send over signs a lease, I'll give them $100 off their next rent payment. While this is a great way to attract new residents, it also reduces the odds of turnover since the person they invite is likely a friend who they'll want to live with for many months to come.

Have a method for interested parties to contact you: either a phone number or a link/QR code to the interest form that we'll discuss later in this chapter.

WRITING YOUR ADVERTISEMENT

When you write the description for your room rental advertisement on the listing site, there are some highlights you should include.

- Benefits provided, including shared supplies, shared space cleaning, utilities, etc.
- Available date
- Bathroom type
- Furnished or unfurnished room
- Furnished shared spaces (living room, kitchen)
- Video tour
- Interest form link (we'll discuss later)

Don't stress too much about writing the description, as I've noticed most potential residents won't read it and will message you with questions instead. Still, spend some time on it for those who do. Below is an example of one of my rental descriptions.

Full-Service Bedroom in Renovated House

Housekeeper cleans shared spaces monthly! Utilities and Wi-Fi provided. All shared supplies such as trash bags, dishwashing pods, paper towels, cleaning supplies, and more are included, so you won't have to worry about running out of essentials. Garage and additional storage space available.

Room Details:

- Bedroom #3 (Available <date>): Room w/ <bath type> Bathroom
- $<rent>/month (Video Tour: <video link>)
All shared spaces—such as the kitchen, living room, and dining room—are furnished.
Cleanings of shared spaces occur monthly, ensuring that the house is always clean and tidy.
The kitchen is newly renovated and includes pots/pans, utensils, plates, bowls, cups, and coffee maker, making cooking and entertaining easy and convenient.
The living room features a large 50" 4K smart TV, and the dining area includes a spacious dining table.

For your convenience, each renter has labeled shelves in the pantry and refrigerator to keep their items separated. Provided shared supplies are restocked as needed. Your bedroom door and the front door are equipped with electronic keypads, enabling further security and convenience. No need to worry about losing your keys; simply use your personal code to lock and unlock the doors. Please let us know if you have any questions; otherwise, please fill out this form if you are interested:
<interest form link>

Storing this description in a document will make it easy to copy and paste to all the various sites you will list on. Some listing sites won't allow links, so you may have to erase the video and interest form links if the website throws an error.

PRICING

The room rental demand test you performed in Chapter 5: Selecting a Market gives you an excellent idea of the room rent in your market. Launching the rooms with shared bathrooms at that rent and those with private bathrooms at 20 percent higher will be a good start. I'd recommend pricing based on your gathered data rather than looking at comparable rooms on the listing services.

When purchasing a property, estimating the value by comparing the subject property to recently sold comparable properties is common. You may think of performing a similar practice to price your rooms by looking at comparable rooms on listing services. I'd discourage this method in favor of using the data you collected during the demand test. When looking at comparable rooms, the listing services do not allow you to look at rooms that have successfully been rented. Instead, you can only look at rooms currently being advertised for rent, so there is no way to tell if the available rooms are priced appropriately. Pricing based on this data can lead you to price too high or too low.

If you aren't filling the rooms as quickly as you'd like, your pricing may need to be adjusted. When I first started renting rooms in my first house hack, I was stubborn with pricing and would hold the rent constant for months if that was what it took to rent the room. This hurt my cash flow in the long run. By keeping a room vacant for three months, I forfeited $2,400. When I finally dropped the rent by $50, I rented the room within a week.

Vacancy is detrimental to your cash flow, so don't hesitate to adjust rent to fill vacancies.

Unfortunately, there isn't currently any dynamic pricing software in the co-living space like there is for short-term rentals. You'll have to adjust the pricing manually for now. There are various ways to adjust your pricing, but I do it based on two factors: how long the room has been listed and the number of vacancies I currently possess across the portfolio.

Each week a room sits vacant, I drop the monthly rate by about $10. This adjustment ensures that, even if I am optimistic about the starting rent, I will eventually hit a sweet spot and snag a resident.

Additionally, I'll adjust rates based on my portfolio vacancy. For example, if I have forty rooms total and eight are vacant because I have recently acquired and listed a property, I'm at a vacancy of 20 percent. I aim to have a 5 percent vacancy or less, meaning I am 15 percent away from my target. To quickly reduce vacancy, I'll lower the price of all rooms by 15 percent. Each time a room gets rented, the vacancy reduces, lowering the discount. Eventually, when I reach only two vacancies, I am now at my target of 5 percent vacancy, so I stop lowering my prices.

Once a room rents, I document the price to use as a reasonable starting rent for the subsequent turnover.

REPLYING TO LEADS

What do you say when leads reach out with the classic "Hi, is this still available?" message. Drafting a new and unique reply each time would be time consuming, so you must take a systematic approach without seeming too cold or corporate.

In the past, I would send a long message about the property and all the benefits with a note at the bottom saying, "Note: We will not reply to messages until the interest form has been filled out. Then we will reply by EMAIL ONLY!" Yeah, that didn't work so well. While I did get some applicants, I was missing out on a good portion due to the length and impersonality of the reply. Now I send a shorter and more pleasant message that outlines a few of the best benefits.

> *Hey <name>!*
> *The place is still available.*
> *We have a number of rooms, so I'm sure one will be perfect for you. Check out this YouTube tour: <video link for the unit they are interested in>*
>
> *A few perks to keep in mind:*
> * *Shared items like toilet paper, trash bags, dishwasher fluid, etc. are provided.*
> * *We have a house cleaner clean the shared spaces monthly.*
>
> *Once you've seen the video, please fill out this form. Let me know if you have any questions!*
> *<interest form link>*

The goal is to have them watch the video tour and become emotionally invested in the room. Then, you want them to fill out the interest form so that you can obtain their information to get an idea of their qualifications.

Some people will continue to ask questions after you send the initial message. In an effort to be personable and build trust, I'll answer a few of their questions, even if they haven't filled out the interest form yet. After a few back-and-forths, though, I'll emphasize that I'd like them to fill out the form before continuing the conversation to prevent either of us from wasting time if they are unlikely to qualify.

Interest Form

The interest form is free and asks the same exact questions as the application. It differs because it is free to fill out and has unverified applicant input. Instead of running a credit report like you would with an actual application, the interest form simply asks, "What do you think your credit is?"

The interest form serves as a sort of pre-application. It can be quickly completed to determine whether the potential resident qualifies for the room. For example, if you only allow one occupant per room and the lead states that they will have two occupants, you can easily screen them out without them wasting money on an application or using your time answering questions and providing tours.

The interest form also serves as an excellent way to collect data. I always ask how the applicant found us. This helps determine which listing services are working the best and which are not. You'll also collect their name, phone number, and email, so even if you select a different applicant for the available unit, you can contact those who filled out the interest form and notify them of future vacancies.

Here is an example of an interest form that you can customize to your liking: www.BiggerPockets.com/CoLivingBonus.

If you are using Google Forms, you can turn on a setting that will notify you each time you get a response. This will allow you to evaluate the submission quickly and respond. Quick response times are essential for keeping a lead interested.

If they appear to pass your criteria, then you can reply (via email or phone) by congratulating them and directing them to your application link. Most property management systems will provide you with one. Do not ignore them if they appear to fail your screening criteria. To treat everyone fairly, you should still reply to them with the application link but mention why they likely wouldn't qualify based on their responses.

Application

The application is the formal submission that describes the quality of the resident. The property management system you use will likely have online application features. We'll talk more about the software you can use in Chapter 14: Tools. The applicant pays for the service, and the fees are used to run background, credit, and eviction checks. Optionally, you can increase the application fee and keep the surplus, but I do not. The purpose of the application isn't to make $10–$20; it is to help you accept or deny an applicant who can bring you thousands of dollars throughout their tenancy.

The application questions are reminiscent of the interest form. Additionally, I like to ask for three previous rental references (name, phone, and email) and uploads of their two latest pay statements from their employer.

When processing the application, you'll compare the results to your screening criteria. Ensure that you process each applicant identically, treating them fairly, to abide by Fair Housing laws. Depending on your criteria, this may include reviewing their income, eviction history, criminal record, credit score, smoker status, and more. Each investor will have unique requirements, but I'd certainly recommend performing the checks specified below.

WEB CHECK

When processing an application, one of the first things I do is perform a web check: I look them up on Google, Instagram, Facebook, and LinkedIn for any possible red flags.

Once, I had an applicant whose background check appeared fine, but upon researching them online, I found out they had been fired from the local school district for embezzling money. This did not appear in the background check because it happened recently, but Google knew. This is not the behavior I'm looking for when deciding who will live with my other residents.

Most applicants are not found in my searches and don't raise red flags, but it's still best to check.

LANDLORD REFERRALS

Landlord referrals are of high importance during applicant screening. Especially in a co-living property, you want to make certain that only high-quality applicants are accepted. If you are managing remotely or don't get the chance to meet the residents personally, speaking with their previous landlords can allow you to discover more about their character and how they might interact with other residents.

Past landlords can be challenging to contact, especially if the resident previously lived at a large apartment complex, but small mom-and-pop operators are usually accessible. I'll email and call the landlords listed to make sure I've made every effort to get in contact. If they don't answer the phone, I'll send a text also. If I still haven't heard back by the following day, I will repeat the process. If I haven't heard from them by the third day, then it is possible I won't and will stop my attempts.

Depending on your local laws, you may be able to adjust the security deposit based on the number of positive rental references you receive. I've found that this is a great way to balance your risk mitigation while lowering the up-front fees the applicant pays. Suppose the applicant does not provide any rental references, or I cannot contact them. In those cases, I'll charge 1.5 times the monthly rent in the form of a security deposit because I don't know anything about their behavior at past rental properties. Often, bad applicants will remove themselves in this case, as they don't want to pay the increased fee. Instead, they'll apply somewhere else that doesn't check landlord references. Contrarily, if I receive three outstanding references, I'll lower the security deposit to 0.5 times the monthly rent since the applicant poses little risk.

When contacting previous landlords, I provide a link to a signed Tenant Information Release Form. This is an electronically signed form from the applicant that gives permission for the landlord to tell me about their experience. Apartments almost always require this form, while independent landlords may not. Just to minimize the back-and-forth with the applicant, I always get it signed at the beginning of the application process, just in case. Then, I'll proceed to ask references these questions:

- Did they pay on time?
- Did they have pets?
- Did they take care of the home?
- Did they give proper notice before vacating?
- Would you rent to them again?

One time, I texted a reference, and he immediately called me back because he wanted to emphasize the extreme issues he had with this applicant. This applicant repeatedly disrespected other residents in the apartment complex. He and his significant other had been behaving inappropriately in plain view of the other residents of the complex. When the property manager confronted him about it, he exclaimed that people could look away if they didn't like it.

Almost all of my applicants have received great reviews from their landlords, but I've dodged some who would have been real nightmares.

Signed Lease

Once an applicant has been fully screened and passes your criteria, you can send them the lease! As a reminder, we discussed the terms you want to include with your lease in Chapter 10: The Lease.

With the number of residents and turnovers you'll experience, you'll undoubtedly want to send and have the lease signed digitally. Most property management software will have online lease-signing abilities, but if not, you can use other online document-signing services.

INITIAL FEES

I require that initial fees be paid after they sign the lease and before moving in. The initial fees include the first month's rent and security deposit.

Let me use some examples to expand upon the first month's rent. If someone signs the lease on September 15 for $800 a month that begins October 1, they must pay an $800 invoice on or before September 30. Their next payment will be on November 1, then December 1, and so on.

The situation becomes more complicated if they start their lease in the middle of the month rather than on the first. Let's say they sign a lease on September 10 to begin September 15. During September, they are only staying for half of the month, so I don't need to charge them the whole $800. Instead, I need to charge them a prorated amount of $400. However, so they have skin in the game, I still want to collect an entire month of rent before they move in, so I'll have them pay a whole month, $800, before moving in on September 15. On October 1, they'll pay the $400. Going forward, on the first day of the month, they will provide the full $800 rent payment. Ultimately, the resident pays the same amount regardless of how the first two payments are treated. But by flipping the first and second months, I receive a larger payment up front, decreasing the odds that they attempt to break the lease if they change their mind close to move-in day.

Before I started flipping those first two payments, I had a lease that began a day before the end of the month, so their first month's rent was 1/30th of a typical payment. They did change their mind and decided not to move in. While I was able to keep their security deposit, plus that smidge of rent, I would have obviously preferred a resident that stayed for six months or longer.

RENTERS INSURANCE

You can require that residents show proof of renters insurance before moving in. Renters insurance covers their personal property in the event of damage and theft. It can also help cover damage to the property caused by the resident if they start a kitchen fire, for example. By requiring that your residents have such a policy, you may reduce headaches and struggles with your insurance in the case of an issue. However, renters insurance claims aren't made very often, so it could be an unnecessary expense and an extra barrier to entry for your residents.

Showings

You may receive requests for tours at any point in the funnel, but I don't allow anyone to tour unless they've submitted and passed the interest form. If they include in their initial message that they would like to request a tour, I tell them they must complete the interest form first to see if they might qualify, preventing them from touring if they don't meet the criteria.

Virtual Tours

You might recall the listing videos I recommended creating in Chapter 8: Furnishing. This is where those come in handy. Videos serve a substantial benefit to the applicants, as many of them are moving from out of state and need housing ready for them upon arrival and do not have the opportunity to do a physical tour. Additionally, video tours reduce the need for time-consuming physical tours since they include the same information that I would relay during a physical tour and show the same spaces. I've found that only 24 percent of applicants have requested to tour the property in person because they consider the video tours sufficient.

As an alternative to videos, you could potentially use a 3D/360° virtual tour service to map your entire property. This may become more common, but I will stick with videos for the foreseeable future. In the videos, I can discuss the property's features and give it the personal touch that a 3D tour would lack.

Here is an example of one of my video tours: www.BiggerPockets.com/CoLivingBonus.

Personal Tours

Some applicants will still want to tour the space in person. If I was an applicant and lived nearby, I'd probably want to see the space, even if a video tour was available. There are various ways in which you can choose to handle in-person tours.

LANDLORD TOUR

The first and obvious option is to provide tours yourself. This option is basically free and allows you to "sell" the room to residents and increase your odds of a successful lease signing. You may also appreciate the opportunity to meet the potential resident and gauge how well they meet your community standards. The downside is that you will have to take time out of your day that, depending on your financial situation, may make more sense to spend on higher-producing activities.

SHOWING AGENT TOUR

Real estate agents, or a trusted individual, can be employed to perform the tour in your place. This is the most expensive option and would cost about $50 per tour. This option saves time for you and can also maintain a sense of professionalism.

EXISTING RESIDENT TOUR

If you already have residents living in the property, why not have them give tours for you? I've found this to be the best option for several reasons.

A current resident providing the tour allows them to meet each other and discern if they are good fits for each other. Additionally, this provides an excellent opportunity for their pet to interact with other residents and other pets, if you allow them, verifying that they all get along. If the introduction reveals that the individual would not fit in well, they'll often screen themselves out or request to visit one of your other available properties. Although you could lose the opportunity to fill a vacancy, this isn't entirely a loss. You want to maintain comfortability in the house, and the presence of a new resident who doesn't enjoy the experience would be harmful.

This option is also less expensive. You could ask current residents to perform tours for free; however, I offer a financial incentive. If the applicant who tours ends up signing a lease, the resident who gives the tour will receive a future rent payment discount, usually $50. Rather than pay for every tour, the discount is only given if the result is a signed lease. This approach aligns the current resident's interests with yours. Despite providing spectacular housing with unmatched amenities, if the current resident has small grievances with their situation, they will be unlikely to mention those and instead focus on all the positives of the property because they want to receive their discount.

To present this incentive opportunity, I email all current residents with a few day and time options that work for the applicant. Once a resident responds and selects a time, I'll connect the two through text, so they are able to make any final arrangements. If the room is vacant, I'll give the current resident a temporary code to enter the room. If it is still occupied, I notify the applicant that they can view the rest of the property aside from the room. If no one replies to the email requests within a day, I'll move on to one of the other options.

If you do not have any residents yet and an applicant requests a tour, you'll have to resort to one of the other options.

SELF-GUIDED TOUR

Another option is to have the applicant tour the property by themselves. This is 100 percent free and requires none of your time. However, it has the lowest odds of resulting in a signed lease due to lack of interaction and additional information. There is also risk of theft or damage to your property.

To help mitigate the risks, I'd only use this option if you have security cameras monitoring all shared spaces of the house.

If you use this option, you'll need to create codes for the front and bedroom doors (if the latter is vacant) and provide them to the applicant. You will also want to give them a strict time frame that the codes will stay active.

Chapter 12

Turnovers

Because of the sheer number of residents, the co-living strategy involves processing numerous move-ins and move-outs. Therefore, it is essential to follow a standard process consistently so critical steps are not overlooked.

Move-In

Once you get a signed lease for a room, you'll want to email the new resident an introduction. In my email, I include:

- Move-in day and time
- Address and unit #
- Parking instructions
- Trash day
- A link to the group chat with the other housemates
- Emergency phone number

Then, I'll send messages to the existing residents of the house, notifying them of the new resident's name, move-in day, and unit number. I also use this message to remind everyone to be kind and welcoming to their new housemate, as they may be nervous to move in.

Next, I'll create their door codes. I ask what they would like their code to be, then I can add that code to the appropriate doors (usually the front door and their bedroom), making it active on their lease start date.

On move-in day, I'll send the introduction email to the new resident again and remind the current residents of their arrival. I do not ask the new resident to complete a move-in checklist, like apartments may, as the room should already be free from any damages. However, you can tell the resident to submit maintenance requests for any overlooked issues, including videos and pictures as evidence.

Move-Out

If you follow the guidance in Chapter 13: Ongoing Management, you'll have done all you can to minimize the frequency of move-out requests; however, move-outs are still inevitable. In fact, move-outs can be something to celebrate! They can signify that you've successfully supported your residents during financially challenging periods of their lives. After all, co-living doesn't have to be a permanent living arrangement for all residents. Ideally, co-living helps residents save money early in their careers, climb the professional ladder with raises and promotions, and eventually transition into more luxurious living accommodations while maintaining their financial health.

If your leases have a fixed end date, you'll want to start these steps as soon as you know the resident is not extending their lease. If they are month-to-month after the end date, you'll want to begin these steps when the resident provides proper notice.

Determine the price at which you will be re-listing the room. If the resident had only been there for six months, the unit will likely rent for a similar amount; however, if it has been occupied for a year or longer, market rents may have gone up. There are a few approaches to calculate this adjustment. You can assume a 3 percent yearly increase since they started renting. Alternatively, if you have other rooms in the area, you can use your recent experience to determine the room's rent. As discussed in Chapter 11: Finding Residents, this is the starting price. Be sure to make adjustments over time until the vacancy is filled.

Now that you know what to price the new listing at, start attracting leads! Of course, you'll advertise the same way you did when you first filled the room, but this is also an excellent opportunity to attract some off-market leads. I like to notify the existing residents of the house about the move-out. In the message, I'll mention that if they have any friends looking for housing, I'll give the resident $100 off next month's rent if the referral successfully signs a lease. Also, I'll email everyone who has filled out the interest form within the past ninety days but decided not to move forward. Many will have found other accommodations, but some will still be looking. Perhaps the location, price, or room features of your previous offerings turned that lead away, but they might be interested in this new opportunity.

When sifting through the new applicants, you should pay attention to their requested move-in date. Accepting someone who wants to move in months after the current resident leaves can result in significant lost rent. You'll want to define a maximum acceptable vacancy period to minimize this.

For example, I will allow for a three-week vacancy between residents. This means I prioritize applicants who can move in within three weeks of the previous resident's departure. As time passes and

I get closer to the end of those three weeks, I adjust the allowable move-in date to be three weeks from the current date. This approach keeps the opportunity somewhat flexible for applicants while ensuring I don't extend the vacancy unnecessarily.

After re-listing the room, I'll send the vacating resident an email to confirm the move-out date and mention their responsibilities:

- Perform a quick clean of their room; the cleaner will do a deeper clean
- Remove food from the kitchen
- Gather personal belongings from shared areas

I'll prorate any future invoices if they are moving out mid-month.

Once they have officially left, I'll disable any door codes they have active (front door, bedroom door, garage door, etc.) so that they no longer have access to the property.

Successfully running a community requires constant optimization and tweaking, so I'll send them a Google Form that allows for anonymous feedback regarding their experience related to their room, the shared areas, and the community. This feedback is helpful for you to make adjustments and provide a better experience to future residents.

The cleaner will visit the property a day after the move-out. The cleaner records a video of the vacating renter's private space so that I have documentation of the move-out condition. Next, any food left by the resident on their designated shelves in the fridge and pantry is removed. The room is then cleaned, along with the private bathroom, if applicable. Last, a final video is recorded of the private space to document the state of the room before the arrival of the next resident.

These videos get uploaded to a Google Drive folder that I have given the cleaner access to, although you can use other cloud storage services. Once uploaded, I'll review them and look for any damages.

I've only seen significant damage once. When the cleaner recorded the video, she pointed out a five-inch-wide hole in the carpet. This was at a house where I was house hacking, and I recalled a recent incident when this may have occurred.

A few months prior, the smoke alarm had gone off in the middle of the night. I went upstairs and told the residents everything was fine in the basement. One resident eagerly replied, "Oh! Must be a false alarm then, definitely a false alarm."

Well, now I know why they promptly brushed it off—they had just burned a hole in the floor and were trying to cover their tracks!

If damages are uncovered when reviewing the videos, you'll want to hire the appropriate service provider to remedy the issues. Provide the previous resident with a description of the damages, pictures and videos before and after the fixes, receipts for the labor and materials, and the final cost that will be deducted from their security deposit.

The entirety of the security deposit is typically returned to the resident, but occasionally some of it must be utilized to ready the room for its next resident. There may be requirements on what you can keep and the time frame in which you must return it.

Chapter 13

Ongoing Management

The most commonly expressed skepticism when I tell investors about co-living is, "That's great, but one house with that many people is too much of a headache for me." Honestly, this is an understandable concern. You probably grew up with three to five people in your house, and you probably had some issues with one of your parents or siblings, so the same should apply in a co-living scenario, right?

Not exactly. It is important to understand that co-living residents aren't your younger brothers or sisters. These are adults looking for a nice, cheap place to live with no fuss.

If you are willing to put in some extra thought and work, you can deploy simple tricks to reduce the chance of conflict within your co-living property.

Remember that you don't have to be the one managing it yourself. In Chapter 9: Management Strategy, we discussed the pros and cons of self-management, third-party management, and in-house management. Regardless of which option you choose, you'll want to ensure the guidance in this chapter is followed by yourself, your third-party manager, or your in-house manager.

Managing While House Hacking

One unique management situation is managing the property while living in it (house hacking). This is a unique twist because you are serving two roles: housemate and property manager.

As a housemate, you live among the other housemates and interact with them daily. You see each other in shared spaces, chat as you pass in the hallway, and probably eat meals or go out together.

As property manager, you protect the investment. This involves assuring a positive community environment, reprimanding those who break house rules, and ensuring rent is paid on time.

These are conflicting roles, as you are half friend and half enforcer. Some may advise you not to tell the housemates that you are the owner and manager in order to disguise yourself. It is very easy for them to uncover that you are the owner and manager if they see a text or email from your personal account, a property tax bill in the mail with your name on it, a post on your social media about the property, or the ownership record on the property accessor's website. Instead, I would encourage you to be honest about the situation, especially since trust would be lost if they find out you've been lying.

The best solution is to be up front with them, stating that this is a business and that the company will always come first. If they do not fulfill their side of the agreement by following the rules and paying rent, you will protect the investment first and foremost. While they are holding up their end of the agreement, there is no issue building a friendship with them.

Provide the Best Experience

I've found that the better experience you provide for your residents, the fewer opportunities for friction among them. The more you provide beyond your competition, the lower the risk of your residents leaving your rental for a competitor. I've seen the benefits of a great experience time and time again. For example, whenever I increase rent for an existing resident, I say in the notice to them: "After evaluating surrounding room rentals, we have decided to increase your rent by $X per month. Remember that while pricing ourselves in line with other room rentals, we provide much more value than any alternatives." I've had very few residents decide to leave due to the increase in rent because the amenities I provide are unmatched.

It's important to remember that there are limits to the experience you can or should provide. For instance, if you had a movie theater and a full-time chef, your residents would stay with you forever! However, such luxurious amenities come with a hefty price tag and would require a rent increase to maintain your cash flow. Therefore, when considering the valuable amenities you can offer your residents, it's crucial to keep in mind that most potential residents are seeking affordable housing. If providing a certain amenity means pricing out your target resident, it's best to pass on it and instead think of more cost-effective ways to enhance their experience.

Shared Supplies

You can probably recall a time when you had housemates and shared a bathroom with another person.

In college, I remember buying a pack of toilet paper for myself to use. I noticed the pack dwindling faster than it should have, as I was the only person who was meant to be using it. Of course, a housemate was using the toilet paper as well. Since I was on a college student budget, that certainly built some resentment. We didn't fight over it, but if enough of those annoyances had built up, we might have found ourselves in a situation involving someone removing themselves from the household. This problem occurs in most co-living properties, but it is easy to fix with some extra expense.

In my properties, I provide supplies commonly shared among the household. These supplies include cleaning spray, dish soap, dishwashing pods, batteries, hand soap, paper towels, toilet paper, and trash bags. Tracking needed supplies, purchasing them, and dropping them off may sound tedious, but in this day and age, it isn't that difficult.

The first step is finding a place to store supplies at the property. You can designate one of the closets in the house as the supply closet, with shelves labeled for each item.

Next, implement a system to determine when a supply is running low. I rely on the residents for this. Initially, I asked them to text us when they were running low on supplies. It was a good starting point, but as the portfolio grew, this became cumbersome and more difficult to keep track of. Now, I post a laminated QR code on the door that sends the resident to a Google Form. On this form, they can select the property they live at and the item they are running low on. You can receive an email notification when there is a new form entry and filter these emails into a specific folder in your inbox. This is a more organized way to collect the supply requests.

Lastly, you must buy the supplies and get them to the residence. Shopping for supplies and dropping them off at your properties could be a part-time job, depending on your scale. Instead, Amazon carries all previously mentioned supplies and will deliver them to the house in two days or less. It might be confusing if some unnamed package shows up at the house, so you can set the receiver name to "Resident: Put in Supply Closet." Any resident who sees the package and reads the label will know what it is and where to put it.

Regarding cost, I spend an average of $500 per year on supplies for each property. If this effort causes even one resident to stay one extra month, it has already paid for itself, and you can expect the provided shared supplies to have a better effect than that.

Do you think your competition is spending the time and money to provide their residents with shared supplies? It's unlikely, and you can easily do it in five minutes or less per month.

House Cleaning

Another excellent service to provide for your residents is house cleaning, which is replete with benefits.

It reduces resident conflict. Imagine seven residents sharing common areas. One resident is bound to be tidier than the rest. Of course, there are rules in place that everyone should follow to clean up after themselves, but even the cleanest resident will occasionally be forgetful. A professional housekeeper will clean those spots and more, making everyone in the house much happier in their spotless environment.

Regular cleanings keep the property in tip-top shape for property tours. Many co-living properties are managed very poorly, and I've heard from prospective residents that other properties they'd toured were disgusting! If you have a well-kept property, it will be at the top of their list.

Cleaners can do a lot more than just keep the home in shape. As discussed in Chapter 12: Turnovers, they can assist with move-ins and move-outs, reducing your time at the property. My cleaners often report maintenance issues, such as broken toilet seats and leaking faucets, ensuring that maintenance doesn't become too delayed.

There are many benefits to having a property cleaner, but how much do they cost, and how often should one visit your property?

As for pricing, it could be less expensive than you think, depending on how much of the property you want cleaned. You certainly want the cleaners to maintain the shared spaces, including the kitchen, living room, shared bathrooms, and hallways. But do they need to clean all of the bedrooms? I typically don't have them clean the private areas, but I offer it as a paid option to my residents. Most residents would prefer to keep their space private, and they typically don't want to spend the extra cash to keep such a small area clean.

If you opt to only have the shared areas cleaned, that is only around half of the house. If a standard house clean in your area is $250, you could expect to pay $125 for just the shared areas. In my experience, it can take several calls to cleaning companies before you find one willing to service such a small area. More often than not, larger companies are not accommodating, but independent cleaners are. I've had the best luck finding these companies through services like Thumbtack and Taskrabbit.

As for frequency, this is up to you. The more often they clean, the cleaner your property will be, but you must be mindful of the cost.

Once your property is 100 percent occupied, I'd suggest having the cleaner do an initial clean. Then, I'd visit the property at two weeks, three weeks, and four weeks to observe when the property starts to get messy. As a reference, I've found that my properties become noticeably dirty toward the end of the fourth week. Testing this in your market is a good idea because it will depend on the resident demographic. I primarily rent to military members, who are typically pretty clean. I'd expect that renting to a different group, like college students, would require a cleaner every two weeks to keep the property in good condition.

Building Community

By default, co-living residents' schedules consist of waking up, going to work, returning home, retreating to their rooms, sleeping, and repeating. While they maintain online friendships and socialize on weekends, they often have minimal interaction with their housemates. This results in an unideal living environment where everyone seems to be shuffling around, avoiding conversations with "strangers." What if you could help bridge the gap and convert these "strangers" into friends?

GROUP CHAT

Creating a group chat is a simple way to encourage community within the house. I'll discuss which software you can use in Chapter 14: Tools, but for now, just know that you won't want to use a text group chat. With residents having different phone brands and people joining and leaving the house often, you'll want something more sophisticated.

Once you select a platform, you can create a chat for each house, then you can send an invite link to all current and incoming residents.

With the group chat in place, residents can easily message each other to schedule their own events, and incoming residents can make introductions before they even move into the house. The chat also allows them to solve more minor issues without involving management. For example, if someone leaves dishes out, a resident can issue a friendly reminder for the other housemates to clean up after themselves rather than tattling by asking management to send an email blast.

HOUSE EVENTS

With a communication system in place, the next layer to promoting community is hosting house events. At these events, folks are encouraged to come out of their rooms and do an activity together to get to know each other. You can get as creative with this as you like, but having a pizza night is a simple place to start.

Pizza nights can be scheduled remotely and don't require your active participation. You can order a 6:30 p.m. delivery of pizzas, notify your existing residents and describe the event, and at 6:30 p.m., everyone will come out of their rooms for some free food and conversation with their housemates.

These events can be performed monthly or quarterly and can be offered in different variations, such as game or movie nights. Don't be afraid to attend some of these events and get to know the people you are providing housing to as well.

By hosting these events, you are enriching the lives of your residents by encouraging them to come out of their shell. If they make even one friend during an event, it can be a game changer for them socially and mentally.

Not only is this beneficial for your residents, but it also saves you money. Yes, you do have to pay for the events, but the more friends each resident makes inside the household, the lower the odds of them wanting to leave your property just to become a stranger in another house again. Creating a space where your residents feel comfortable can be a win-win, which is what good landlords strive for.

In fact, in my own house hack, the housemates and I rarely spoke to each other. We'd pass each other in the hallway and politely say hello, but we didn't know each other. That all changed when I hosted the first event a year after we all moved in together: a pizza night. I thought we'd spend thirty minutes casually chatting, but instead, we spent over an hour and a half laughing and getting to know each other, exceeding my expectations. During the following weeks, residents started being more interactive in the group chat and shared spaces, and one of the residents even started baking once a week for everyone. That single event positively changed the environment of the house forever.

The Little Things
You can do plenty of other things to make your property the best co-living experience in your market. I'll cover some ways that I enhance the experience, but I encourage you to brainstorm other ideas, test them out, and survey your residents to see how it affects them.

LABELING SHARED SPACES

Another great way to improve the experience is to assign refrigerator and pantry shelves to each unit. This removes any confusion about how much space each person is allowed and reduces the stress on each resident. When they first move in, they don't have to worry about moving everyone else's food to make space for their own. Additionally, it makes it easier to maintain a clean fridge and pantry because the cleaner can sweep all of the contents of the outgoing resident's shelf into the trash upon move-out.

UTILITIES

In traditional long-term rentals, it is common for the residents to register their own internet, water, sewer, electricity, and trash companies to service the property. This would be a confusing way to go about these services in the case of co-living.

When I was in college, some friends and I rented a property together, and one of the moms registered the internet. We all just paid her every month. This was great, until her son moved out in the summer, and I lost access to the internet in the middle of the day. Luckily, I siphoned off the neighbor's Wi-Fi for the rest of the summer, but it was still inconvenient.

You have the flexibility to choose how to handle utility payments by either paying the utilities yourself or splitting the costs and billing them back to the residents.

Billing the residents back for utilities decreases your expenses for a little extra work. You will have to decide how each utility is split. Is water split based on the number of rooms? Is electricity and gas split based on the size of the rooms? Is the internet split based on the amount of data used?

Paying the utilities yourself is a straightforward option that can bring peace of mind to all involved. For the landlord, it eliminates the need to spend time splitting bills and accounting for prorations. For the residents, it simplifies their responsibilities, as they only have one payment to make. This approach also reduces potential friction among residents, as all utilities are covered by the landlord, regardless of usage.

A mix of the previous two approaches is to charge a flat utility fee. You can estimate what utilities cost monthly and split the cost among the rooms you have. If you have any vacancies, you may not have the total fees required to cover the utilities for that month since the fee is fixed; however, you will have more income, offsetting the utility expense. Additionally, issues between residents will be reduced, as everyone is paying an equal amount no matter how long one housemate spends in the shower.

When you pay for the utility bill or charge flat fees, you risk being stuck with a hefty bill when residents are not mindful of their usage. In some situations, you may be able to discover who is misusing the utilities and bill them back, but most of the time, you'll just have to foot the bill since it is difficult to place the blame. If you notice gross misuse repeatedly, you can confront the entire house and suggest that utilities will start being charged back to the residents if the usage doesn't come under control.

LAWN CARE

The grass, bushes, and trees must be trimmed and maintained. One thing is certain: Only one person should be responsible for the lawn maintenance. If it is everyone's responsibility, then it is no one's. Should you have a particular resident be responsible for the lawn care, or should you hire a professional?

Some co-living investors select an existing resident to maintain the lawn in exchange for reduced rent. I am opposed to this for a couple of reasons. First, you'd likely need to supply the equipment, increasing your start-up costs. Second, it adds a point of failure to your management process. Eventually, a resident will slack on this job, souring the relationship between you two and potentially losing that resident and their rent. Third, I'm not a lawyer, but I'm sure there are some liability concerns with having a resident operating a machine, with many sharp blades spinning at 3,000 RPM, to maintain your yard.

For these reasons, I prefer to hire a professional to maintain the lawn. If that company starts to slack, I can fire them and hire someone else, but I won't lose a resident who brings in $800 a month.

SNOW REMOVAL

In markets that regularly receive snow, the risk of a resident or neighbor slipping and falling increases as snow accumulates at the property, especially on concrete surfaces like the sidewalk and driveway. To mitigate this risk, you'll want to consider your options for snow removal.

First, check your local ordinances. If it states that the residents are responsible for snow removal, you can consider providing supplies for the house, such as a snow shovel and snow melt. If you do this, mention in the lease that residents are responsible for removing snow in accordance with the local ordinances. With multiple people in the house, you'll want to message the residents and ensure someone fulfills this responsibility, potentially discounting their rent. This solution can work well for cities where it snows a few times each year, but it isn't a constant occurrence in the winter.

If your city requires snow removal be the owner's responsibility, or if it assigns the responsibility to residents but snowfall is frequent, hiring a professional snow-removal service is a good option. This is an additional expense, but it is worth it for the safety of your residents and the reduction of lawsuit risk. Be sure to shop around, though, as some companies will price per visit, and some will price for the season. Depending on the weather in your city, one may be more cost-effective than the other.

House Rules

In your childhood or current home, how smoothly would things run if there were no rules? The house would be a mess, everyone would be irritated at each other, and no one would want to live there. How can an investor expect multiple people to coexist without standard rules for everyone to follow?

Most of the rules are common sense, but common sense is less common than it sounds. Each resident has a different background and living habits. A housemate may not have bad habits, but they may be distinct enough from other residents that some friction begins to occur. One person may leave their breakfast dishes in the sink until after dinner, when they wash everything. Someone else may clean all their cookware immediately, before even eating their food. One of the residents is likely to form some resentment against the other one, although they are just cleaning dishes like they always have.

I presented some rules and regulations in Chapter 10: The Lease, but below, we will go into more detail regarding the rules I find to be of utmost importance. Although they are listed in the lease, everyone forgets about them within a few weeks of moving in. I'd recommend printing these rules on nice laminated sheets and placing them in relevant areas throughout the house. For example, post sheets with bathroom rules in each shared bathroom, kitchen rules in the kitchen, and general rules for the house in the entryway. These posted sheets can also be an excellent place to put other important information like the Wi-Fi details and emergency contact phone number.

You can find an example of my nicely formatted house rules here: www.BiggerPockets.com/CoLivingBonus.

Kitchen Rules

The most important rules apply to the kitchen. These rules guide how dishes should be washed (dishwasher or hand-washed) and how often they should be washed. If you have a dishwasher, be sure to advise the residents *not* to pull a singular, clean dish out of the dishwasher as needed. This will result in the dishwasher being half clean and half dirty all the time. If you don't have this rule now, you will after all the complaints from residents accidentally drinking from dirty glasses. I ask that anyone who pulls a clean dish from the dishwasher unload it entirely.

Rules concerning the cleanliness of the stove, oven, and microwave are important as well. Residents should always clean up any messes created while using a cooking appliance.

Provide guidance regarding kitchen trash. If a resident throws trash away and the bag is full enough that the lid doesn't shut, they should be respectful of their housemates and take it out and replace the bag.

Bathroom Rules

Shared bathrooms can be a common source of conflict, as multiple housemates will likely share them. Rules regarding bathroom cleanliness are easier to enforce if you provide the right supplies, like cleaning sprays, plungers, and toilet brushes. With those tools provided, they should be capable of maintaining bathroom cleanliness. Similarly to the kitchen trash, residents should remove the bathroom trash and replace the bag once it is full.

Quiet Hours and Guests

Quiet hours and guest rules are necessary for properties with shared living spaces. Most residents work during the day and sleep at night, so my quiet hours are defined as 10 p.m. to 9 a.m. Out of respect for all housemates, the entire house should be silent between these hours: No TV, music, or voices should be heard outside of private bedrooms.

A guest policy is equally important. I've talked with landlords who allow guests at any time, and some do not allow guests at all. In my case, I want to enable residents to have guests over with some limits. After all, this is their home, and it should feel like it. Giving them freedoms like these increases the odds that they stay longer, lowering vacancy and increasing cash flow.

Smoking and Pet Policies

In traditional long-term rentals, pets are often allowed, and smoking is sometimes allowed. In a co-living scenario, you need to consider how these policies will affect the health and safety of all residents at the property.

Not only can the smell of smoke annoy other residents, but it can also introduce respiratory issues and other safety hazards, including fires. I'd recommend not allowing smokers at your property due to these risks to your property and residents.

Allowing pets can also introduce issues. There is the risk of a pet attacking another resident, and the risk of allergies is even more likely. A substantial portion of the population has allergies to certain types of animals. Even if the existing residents don't mind if a pet is introduced, you never know if a future resident will have allergies. If you don't discriminate against pets when screening, then you may have to discriminate against a potential applicant who has allergies. For this reason, I wouldn't recommend allowing free-roaming pets. However, you could allow pets, like fish or snakes, that stay in the resident's room. If you choose to allow free-roaming pets, make sure you notify all existing and future residents of the situation; otherwise, you might find yourself in a sticky situation.

Handling Conflict

While I've given you lots of guidance on how to prevent conflicts from occurring within the house, they will still happen from time to time. The most common conflicts you'll encounter involve residents leaving their things in the living room, making a mess in the kitchen, being noisy at night, having guests over too often, or stealing food from the fridge or pantry.

On rare occasions, you may encounter more severe, pressing issues, like violence. If the residents have not contacted the police, that is the first action you should take. Then, proceed with the steps below as with any other issue.

Regardless of the severity of the problem, you should document it with as much evidence and detail as possible. If you choose to install cameras in the shared areas, as discussed in Chapter 8: Furnishing, you can use the captured footage as undeniable evidence. If you do not have cameras and the problem is still ongoing, like with shared space cleanliness, you can send someone to the property to capture pictures and videos or ask current residents to send you pictures and videos. For intermittent issues that are difficult to capture, like food theft, unfortunately, if you don't have cameras, you'll probably just have testimony from the other residents.

Once you have documented the issue thoroughly, notify the offending resident and provide the documentation. Depending on the severity of the issue, you may give them an opportunity to remedy their mistake or immediately give them options for leaving the community. If it is something less severe, like a cleanliness issue, and you offer them an opportunity to fix it, be sure to tell them how many more chances they have before they'll be asked to leave the community.

If you do reach the stage where the best solution is for the resident to exit the property, you have a couple of options.

First, if their lease term expires soon or they are on a month-to-month lease, you may be able to wait a short period and then just not renew their lease. In most states, there are regulations about how far in advance you must notify the resident before not renewing their lease or even rules about why you can refuse to renew it, so research this before pursuing this option.

Next, you can ask them to leave voluntarily. If you provided the evidence I suggested, the resident will likely accept this solution. I've had success with asking them to leave within a week, penalty-free. Unfortunately, you may have a more extended vacancy than expected since you have little time to refill the room, but that is just a cost of doing business.

If they do not agree to leave, you can offer "cash for keys" by offering them a sum of money in exchange for them peacefully vacating. This may sound ridiculous, but paying them one to two months' rent is much cheaper than eviction.

Lastly, if they still do not agree to vacate, you'll have to start the eviction process. Evictions can be quite complicated, so I'd recommend hiring a law firm that specializes in them. Not only are they more experienced with evictions than other types of lawyers, but they are often cheaper since they have systems set up to process many evictions efficiently.

Property Upkeep

Property upkeep is crucial in a co-living property to prevent it from catching on fire, flooding, or deteriorating until it becomes a health hazard.

Let's start by distinguishing repairs and maintenance from capital expenditures, since they are often confused.

Repairs and maintenance are the responsibility of the landlord or tenant, depending on the severity and location of the issue. This involves servicing systems to extend their life, fixing broken systems, and making minor replacements. Examples include swapping the furnace filter, fixing the refrigerator, and replacing a burned-out light bulb.

Capital expenditures are the landlord's responsibility. These involve replacing major systems, such as the roof, the water heater, and the furnace.

For the most part, your major systems that require capital replacement don't deteriorate faster just because many people live in the house, so you'll treat these like you would in a traditional, long-term rental. Repairs and maintenance, however, are treated uniquely in a co-living property.

Determining Emergency or Nonemergency

You must be able to distinguish between an emergency and a nonemergency, as the response to each is entirely different.

I consider an emergency to be any issue threatening a resident's safety or causing significant damage to the property. Examples include major water leaks, gas leaks, HVAC failures, and fires.

I consider a nonemergency any issue that still requires attention but does not pose an immediate threat to a resident or the integrity of the property. Examples include broken garbage disposals, dripping faucets, and nonfunctioning electrical outlets.

Emergency Repairs and Maintenance

First, you need to have a process for receiving emergency requests from residents, and the residents need to be aware of the process. In my case, I have a phone number that my residents can call anytime with emergencies. This phone number is posted at the property, and I send emails every month reminding all residents to save the number to their phones.

Equally important is having a well-defined process for handling emergency requests. Maintaining a list of local contractors and knowing which ones to contact for specific issues is a surefire way to ensure quick and correct responses to an emergency. Before I even receive a request, I've already prepared a detailed plan for each potential emergency, including whom to contact and whether other residents need to be informed. For instance, if a resident reports a gas leak, I immediately contact the local gas leak emergency line and notify all residents, advising them to vacate the premises without delay.

By preparing for these emergencies, you'll worry much less knowing you are prepared for the worst.

Nonemergency Repairs and Maintenance

Similar to emergency repairs and maintenance, you need a process for receiving and handling nonemergencies, though you'll want to ensure your process won't wake you up in the middle of the night. I recommend receiving them through your property management software or text message. Through these channels, you can respond more flexibly and in a less timely manner. Also, you can receive pictures and videos that help describe the issue.

I process these requests differently than emergency requests and split them into urgent and nonurgent requests.

Urgent requests are not considered threatening, like an emergency, but they could cause major inconvenience for a resident to live without for an extended period of time. Examples include nonfunctioning bedroom lights, missing toilet seats (yes, this happens), and broken microwaves. These requests should be taken care of urgently.

Nonurgent requests are minor annoyances that residents could deal with for some time. Examples include sticking doors, dripping faucets, and slow-draining sinks or tubs.

Nonemergency, urgent maintenance requests should be handled promptly. For the most part, though, you'll mostly receive nonemergency, nonurgent requests. Initially, I sent a repair person to my properties multiple times per week to fix nonurgent issues. The fees for these visits began to accumulate, so now I batch these fixes by adding them to a running list. That list is periodically relayed to the repair person so they can make multiple fixes in one trip.

Recurring Walk-Throughs

With traditional, long-term rentals, it is common for the landlord to go years without seeing the inside of their property until a vacancy occurs. While this may be fine for long-term rentals, it can devastate your co-living business.

With a long-term rental, does the tenant care if they make a mess and attract ants? If that is how they want to live, that is totally up to them. In a co-living situation, would the majority of residents who clean up after themselves care if one resident makes a mess in their room and attracts ants? Yes, they would! But how will you know if residents are treating their rooms with respect? You won't, unless you perform walk-throughs on the property.

This is also an opportune time to take proactive steps to keep your property in tip-top shape, enhancing the experience for your residents and reducing future maintenance issues.

What is a recurring walk-through? This is a monthly, quarterly, or biannual period when you enter your property and evaluate its status. I notify the residents of the walk-through, making them aware that their presence is not mandatory. Then, I do a quick walk-through of the entire house: living room, kitchen, bedrooms, bathrooms, etc. I want to ensure residents don't leave food in their rooms, don't have free-roaming pets, and are following all other house rules.

This is also a great time to check on the property's systems and perform any necessary maintenance. I have a Google Form when walking the property with a task list for things like swapping the AC/furnace filter, checking the water heater for leaks, changing smart lock batteries, checking for leaks under sinks, checking for slow drains, testing all smoke detectors, etc.

If I didn't do these walk-throughs, some issues could get out of hand. Eventually, a resident would alert me, but how much damage would it have caused in the meantime? By proactively looking for issues, I prevent future headaches and costs down the road.

In fact, a few months ago I had an $800 water bill at a property due to three running toilets. Fortunately, these issues were discovered during a walk-through and fixed halfway through that month; otherwise, the bill would have been $1,600.

Remember that nonurgent, nonemergency running maintenance list I mentioned? I also make sure to have all those issues remedied during this visit. So, instead of going to the property to replace the broken door stopper on Monday and tighten the loose towel rack on Thursday, all of these minor fixes are batched and taken care of in one visit, saving time and money.

This is an excellent task to outsource. Doing the walk-throughs yourself could consume days of your time, especially once you have more than a few properties. Instead, you can have an assistant follow the checklist or Google Form for you. I have them record the video walk-through and send it to me so I can review it remotely. You may be averse to paying someone to spend two hours at your property, but you are likely to come out ahead if you discover one leaky water heater that is about to cost you $1,500 in basement repairs. Then you'll be happy you spent $80 on a walk-through, and your residents will be too.

Responsibility

Repairs and maintenance are primarily the responsibility of the landlord. If there is a hole in a bedroom wall, then you know which resident is responsible and can charge them for the repair. But, if there is a stain on the floor in the living room, how can you prove which resident spilled their milkshake and make them remedy the issue? Even if you have cameras in the shared spaces, it can be difficult. Fortunately, by buying and operating your property correctly, you'll be making a lot of cash flow with this strategy, so you should be able to scrape a portion off the top and fill your reserves for dealing with such issues.

Additional Income Opportunities

Unique to co-living, there are some additional ways that you can generate income beyond just renting the bedrooms.

Spend some time thinking about what is in limited supply at your house. What is at the property that only one of the residents can use? That could be turned into an additional income stream. Thus far, I've identified two amenities in limited supply at many of my properties that are in high demand by the residents.

Garage spaces are highly sought after in my market, primarily because it is in a hail zone. Since there is a lot of demand from residents to keep their vehicles free from damage, and a limited supply of garage spaces, I can charge for it and increase my cash flow. I initially listed a garage space at $80 a month, and it was immediately claimed. Then I tried $100 a month. Again, it was immediately taken. I've since played around with the pricing and found that $120 a month is a good price point that the residents are often willing to pay for a single garage spot. If you have a two-car garage, that is an extra $240 a month or $2,880 a year in cash flow just by renting something that already existed at your property!

Many of my properties have storage sheds in the backyard. Since I don't allow residents to store their items in shared spaces, many like the extra space. Similar to the parking, I tested different prices and found that $50 a month was often worth the cost to residents. This is $600 a year in additional cash flow!

I've only scratched the surface of additional amenities that can be offered. More ideas include renting room furnishings and renting office space in the house.

Be a Great Landlord

In summary, there are no standard rules for managing a co-living property. This strategy is still in its early days, so it is up to you to decide how to manage it.

The standard I've set in this chapter is high. I understand that many of the additional services cost money; however, they enhance the lives of the residents living in your properties. Ultimately, yes, residents do generate income for you, but they aren't cash cows. They are human beings and deserve a safe, well-maintained space to live in, surrounded by a community that feels like a family.

In business, the most valuable deals benefit all parties. If you can generate significant cash flow while providing an exceptional living experience, you've achieved a true win-win scenario and have a solid business model.

Chapter 14

Tools and Resources

Now that you've learned how to buy, set up, and manage a co-living property, it's important to prepare yourself for the challenges ahead.

Especially if you plan to scale, now is the time to equip yourself with the right tools and resources to streamline your processes, save time, and set you up for long-term success. I've sprinkled information throughout this book about tools and software that can assist you, but now let's take a deep dive into the tools you should have to make co-living more effortless and organized.

Don't let picking your favorite software, setting it up, and learning how to use it stall your progress. That is why this chapter sits toward the end of the book rather than the beginning. It is easy to set everything up and feel productive when you are actually procrastinating. Consider setting up a few of these tools while buying your first property and layering on the rest once you've purchased a few properties.

Similarly, don't worry too much about non-income-producing activities like creating a website or obtaining a business email address in the early days. While these may be useful in the future, using your personal email address will be sufficient for your first few properties, and maybe beyond.

I'll discuss the types of tools and what they are helpful for, but for the most part, I won't specify any particular tools. The landscape is constantly changing as platforms are updated and new competitors join the fold, so you can find my latest recommendations for specific software tools here: www.BiggerPockets.com/CoLivingBonus.

General Tools and Resources

Some tools are very specific and are only helpful for a focused purpose, like a drill bit. It is only useful for drilling a hole of a particular size. Other tools are useful for many purposes, like a hammer. A hammer can drive nails when building a wall, pry nails to undo a mistake, and bust down a wall that is no longer needed. The general tools I discuss in this section are like the hammer—helpful across your business for various purposes.

Financial Management System

Many new investors overlook the importance of managing their finances. Closely watching your finances serves two important purposes: documenting your financials for your accountant and tracking your property's actual performance. A great bookkeeping software will help you with both.

Your bookkeeping software connects to your bank accounts and credit cards to pull in all transactions automatically. Then, you can upload receipts for each expense and assign them to the correct property and category.

For example, let's assume you have two properties. The incoming rent, mortgage payments, and utility bills will be imported for these properties. You can then attach the receipts, connect them to the right property, and categorize the transactions appropriately. Then you can review your actual cash flow for each property.

Many investors focus on calculating what they expect cash flow to be before purchasing the property and neglect the actual performance once it is owned. To be a great investor, you'll need to track the performance of your properties and use the data to make decisions. For example, if you notice that cash flow for a particular property is dipping, you may wonder why. Upon further investigation in your bookkeeping software, you may find that the water bill is extremely high, indicating that some residents are being wasteful or there is a leak somewhere on the property.

Additionally, your accountant must have a financial picture of all your properties at tax time. Rather than scrambling to find your receipts from over the entire year at tax time, you can click a button to send your accountant all the income and expense information you've been tracking, making tax time much less stressful.

Hiring a bookkeeper can be relatively inexpensive, if this doesn't sound like something you want to do yourself. Remember that you'll still need to send receipts to them and may have to explain what each expense is for, but they can do the rest of the heavy lifting.

Task Management System

As I've discussed extensively throughout the book, you should document all your tasks, store that information, reference it the next time you perform the task, and improve the process.

While I've provided you with all my methods for acquiring, setting up, and managing co-living properties, the best practices may change over time. You may find ways to build on my systems. A task management system will allow you to store all these processes, systems, and checklists as you improve.

Task management software is basically a glorified reminders app that allows you to create checklists, attach videos, set due dates, and save templates for repeatable processes. As your co-living business grows, I encourage you to record your processes. This will enable you to assign the tasks to a team member once they are onboarded. Rather than spending many hours training them, you can save time by providing them with the process you've created and refined.

Document Management System

Real estate involves abundant paperwork, including signed offers, purchase agreements, and leases. You'll need somewhere to store all of these documents. While you can store them on your computer, it is risky, as your computer can fail at any time. Instead, I'd recommend storing all business documents remotely with a reliable cloud storage provider.

In addition to storing documents, you'll need a place for some of your service providers to upload videos. For example, you'll want your cleaner to upload videos of the rooms upon move-out and your repair person to upload videos of the property walk-throughs.

In the past, I would ask these videos to be texted to me, but this became cumbersome, as the video quality suffered. Now, I have the videos uploaded directly to the appropriate folder through a provided link to preserve video quality and keep everything organized.

Acquisitions Tools and Resources

As you build your co-living portfolio, having the right tools becomes essential to repeatedly making informed decisions and staying organized. These resources will help you accurately calculate returns, efficiently track leads, and streamline the acquisition process.

Lead Sources

As you scale your acquisitions, you'll need more and more sources of leads. As discussed in Chapter 6: Finding the Ideal Property, these leads can either be on market or off market. Each type of lead will have its sources.

On-market leads will come straight from your real estate agent or an MLS clone, like Zillow or Redfin. Interacting directly with this data through the web portals works well, but tools can help you download all the listings in bulk to review the current offerings more quickly and efficiently. The tool you select should offer options to download all the current listings as a spreadsheet, so they can be entered into your lead tracking system.

Off-market leads can be tricky to find as, by definition, they are off the market and not publicly listed. Henry Washington's book, *Real Estate Deal Maker* (www.BiggerPockets.com/ReadDealMaker), discusses all the sources where you can find these leads. To simplify things, you can use data aggregation tools that present potential off-market leads, although they will be lower quality than uncovering them firsthand, as Henry teaches. Such tools are still helpful, though, if you need lots of lead flow and do not have the time to spend directly sourcing the leads. These data aggregators should offer a web portal where you can filter properties based on ownership status, equity amount, distress level, and more. Additionally, they should provide contact methods for reaching the owner (phone numbers, emails, and mailing addresses).

Lead-Tracking System

Once you have on- and off-market leads coming across your desk, you need a way to organize them and track their status. A simple spreadsheet often does the trick, where you can customize data for each lead. You'll likely want columns for the address, bed and bath count, asking price, square footage, estimated performance metrics, offers sent, and follow-up date.

Furthermore, there are more advanced tools than spreadsheets that offer features like automatically fetching the estimated property value, integrating with email or phone systems to log communication, and more.

Deal Analysis Tool

As discussed in Chapter 6: Analyzing and Making Offers, deal analysis is the final step before submitting an offer on the property. As such, it's vital to estimate your future returns to a high degree of accuracy. To do this, you'll need to select a reliable tool to run the numbers for you. A great start is using a tool like the BiggerPockets Rental Property Calculator. This tool has been tested hundreds of thousands of times and is almost guaranteed to produce the correct results, given the proper inputs.

At some point, you may want to create a spreadsheet you can customize specifically for your acquisitions. However, before using it to purchase a property, you should rigorously test its results against a reliable tool.

Remodel Tools and Resources

Planning a remodel for co-living properties involves understanding the existing layout and designing a new one that maximizes the space's potential. The right tools can make this process far more efficient and precise, ensuring that your remodel aligns with your vision for the property.

Floor Plan Capturing

One of the worst parts about initially planning your remodel is figuring out the property's current floor plan. Flipping through photos of the property on the listing platform can often leave you confused, as it cuts from the living room on the main floor to the bedroom on the upper floor, to the game room in the basement, and back to the living room on the main floor. Sometimes, you'll find a virtual tour or floor plan attached to the listing, but if not, you or your real estate agent will have to visit the property to determine exactly how everything is laid out.

Today there are phone apps that you or your agent can download that use your phone's camera to create a pretty accurate floor plan of the house. By walking around the inside of the property and scanning each area with the phone, the tool will return a floor plan, with measurements, of each property level. Such a tool is vital for co-living properties where you are likely adding bedrooms and bathrooms, and knowing the positioning of the existing walls is paramount.

Floor Plan Designing

Once you know the existing floor plan, if you add bedrooms and/or bathrooms, you'll need to design a new floor plan with your additions. This doesn't have to be an architectural drawing. Instead, you just need to capture the general idea for your contractor.

Unless you want to get super detailed, simply drawing lines depicting where the new walls should go often suffices. For extensive floor plan modifications you can use tools to recreate the existing floor plan and make all of your proposed changes. The great thing about these tools is that you can quickly visualize different scenarios. For example, you could see whether converting a basement into two smaller bedrooms or one large bedroom with its own bathroom makes the most sense.

Management Tools and Resources

Managing co-living properties can be manual and exhausting, but the right tools can make management far easier. In this section, we'll explore tools, like property management software and communication platforms, that can streamline operations, improve resident satisfaction, and save you time.

Property Management Software

Property management software (PMS) is essential. Gone are the days of handling paper applications and mailing letters to residents. These days, an online PMS will assist with 80 percent of your workload, so it is a critical category.

A great PMS should streamline the application process. The applicant can fill out the application in the software, providing their personal information, rental reference contact information, and pay statements. The system should then automatically run the background, credit, and eviction checks and return the results to you.

The PMS should have online lease-signing features too. In particular, you should be able to upload your lease and have the fields prefilled for the accepted applicant. Rather than manually typing their name in the fields, including the address, rent amount, and security deposit amount, the system should be smart enough to pull all that information in for you. Then, you and the resident should be able to sign entirely online without meeting in person to sign physical documents.

Your PMS will also handle all rent collection. Ideally, the resident will have multiple options within the system to submit their payment, usually by bank account or debit/credit card. While I don't want residents to use a credit card to pay their rent regularly, they sometimes get in a pinch, and this option can help both of us. All payments are directly sent to your bank account, although the processing times can vary based on the PMS. Additionally, the PMS should be able to apply late fees automatically if rent is overdue.

The PMS should provide a maintenance portal where residents can submit requests with a description of the issue and an option to upload photos and videos. The ticket can be assigned to the maintenance tech you choose, providing them with all the information they'll need.

The cost of the software will vary. Some PMSs are totally free, while others charge a flat monthly fee, a fee based on the number of units, or a fee for each transaction.

Communication Platform

To provide an exceptional community experience, you'll want to have some means of communication for the property. While text group chats could technically work, a more feature-rich solution is ideal.

Whichever platform you choose should be able to host individual and group chats. Group chats will be essential for the housemates to communicate with each other. When you have multiple properties in the same city, you can even have a huge group chat with all residents to expand the community.

While group chats are helpful for your residents to communicate with each other, you can also use them to announce community events and other important updates.

You can communicate with residents through the communication platform by messaging them directly. I've found that many of my residents had been willing to communicate over email during the application process, but once they had moved into the house, they paid less attention to their email. The communication platform will behave similarly to a text message, displaying a notification to the resident on their phone as soon as a message is received, increasing the odds that they see it and enabling a much quicker reply.

Part V

Co-Living for Advanced Investors

Chapter 15

Why and When to Scale

While the acquisition, setup, and management of co-living properties get easier with repetition, new problems will emerge as you scale your portfolio to five, ten, or twenty-plus properties. A portfolio of such size involves a more advanced layer of investing that if not developed properly will likely cause your business to fail.

That may sound eerie, but it is the truth. Plenty of investors created a solid, small portfolio with good returns, only to get too excited too quickly and cause the whole thing to implode on their way to becoming multimillionaires. To prevent you from making such mistakes, let's first determine if you even want to scale your portfolio and, if so, how you know if you are ready to scale it appropriately with less risk.

Why Scale

An obvious reason you may want to scale is that, if done correctly, the larger your portfolio becomes, the more cash flow you will have. This can lead to more freedom, vacations, toys, and charitable giving. Also, since this strategy often focuses on providing more affordable housing to those struggling financially, the more rooms you offer, the more people you can help.

Furthermore, the larger your portfolio becomes, the better economies of scale. This just means that the cost per property or person should decrease for certain services. For example, when I had two properties, I paid the cleaner $120 for each property cleaning. As I acquired more properties, I asked if I could have a cheaper rate if I brought her more business. She agreed. This is a total win-win. I now pay her $100 for each property cleaning—a win for me, because it is less than I used to pay. Instead of making $240 for two cleanings, she makes $600 for the six properties I've given her, which is also a win. Similar scales can apply to lawn care and repair services.

Scaling also further spreads your risk. If you recall, co-living offers less risk than strategies that house a single resident because multiple residents are paying rent, meaning if one doesn't pay, you still collect most of your rent. Similarly, the more properties you have, the more income sources you have, and the more opportunity for your income sources to successfully pay you.

While all of these benefits of scale are great, and it further spreads out your risk, your overall risk can be higher, especially if you are not equipped to scale at this time.

When to Scale

By this point, you know how to purchase and operate a co-living property very well, but just because you've done it once or twice doesn't mean you are ready to add more. There are additional considerations. If certain conditions are unmet, you could be scaling straight into a failing business. Let's determine if now is the right time for you to scale with high odds of success.

Reserves

In the initial stages of your portfolio, especially if you have other income, a lack of reserves won't kill you. In these stages, your income can likely support a few repairs, replacing the water heater, and a vacancy. Depending on the amount of other income, when you reach a certain property threshold, it becomes difficult to pay for these costs out of your pocket.

For example, let's assume that water heaters cost $1,500, all appliances cost $3,500, and flooring costs $15,000. Also, let's assume each item needs to be replaced, on average, every seven years. That means that, statistically, you'll need to pay $20,000 over seven years to keep the property in functional condition. When averaged over the seven years, that is only $2,850—probably coverable with any other income you have, even if you haven't prepared reserves.

Now imagine you have seven properties. Across the portfolio, statistically, you'll have to pay $20,000 annually because a water heater will likely go out at one house, the appliances at another, and flooring at another. Using your other income to cover $20,000 of expenses every year is much more difficult! That is why reserves become much more important as you scale.

How much in reserves should you have? If you recall from Chapter 6: Analyzing and Making Offers, repairs and maintenance are not very costly and happen regularly. These can easily be covered by the rent your residents pay, so you don't need to consider this when determining how much to have in reserves. On the other hand, capital expenses involve replacing more expensive items over more extended periods. Since the cost is higher and you are unsure when the expense will occur, you'll need reserves to cover them safely.

As discussed, capital expenses can cost about 7.5 percent of the annual gross income, so you should at least build your reserves to 7.5 percent of the annual income you expect from your portfolio. However, when you have a few properties, I'd recommend saving up more than that because you don't have a large enough sample size for that 7.5 percent per year to be strictly true.

With a smaller portfolio, you may spend 5 percent in one year, then 10 percent, then 9 percent, then 6 percent on capital expenses. Over those four years, you averaged 7.5 percent. However if you had exactly 7.5 percent in your reserves, you wouldn't have enough to cover the expenses in the second and third years. In those earlier stages, you need to pad your reserves more. As you add more properties to your portfolio, you will get closer and closer to hitting the 7.5 percent on the dot. Thus, you'll need to pad the reserves less over time.

Figure 15 shows the statistical reserves needed (assuming 7.5 percent for capital expenditures). I'd consider this the absolute minimum you should have. You'll also see the padded reserves. I recommend building to this level before adding another property to your portfolio. The buffer for the padded reserves exponentially decreases over time. By property number seven, the gap between the padded and statistical reserves mostly closes, so at that point, you are pretty safe assuming 7.5 percent.

Recommended Reserves

— Statistical Reserves   · · · Padded Reserves
− − Property Count (Assuming $70,000 income/property)

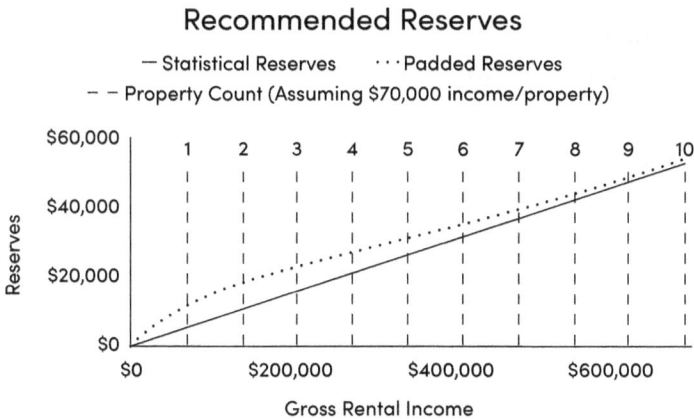

Figure 15. Recommended reserves for a co-living portfolio

Capital

Once you know you have the appropriate reserves, you'll want to ensure you have enough capital to purchase another co-living property. Suppose it has been a while since you last bought, and you are unsure how much capital you'll need to close, remodel, and furnish the property. In that case, you'll probably want to analyze a handful of currently available properties to estimate how much you'll need. If you recently purchased a property similar to what you would buy again, you can assume a similar amount of capital will be required.

Capital is probably the biggest constraint investors have. If you don't have enough capital, you'll either need to wait to save up more or consider partnering. We'll talk about partnerships in Chapter 17: More Money.

Time

Do you have time to purchase and manage more properties? As for the acquisitions, you can expect to spend at least a few hours per week reviewing the latest leads that enter your funnel. As for the management, if you are still self-managing, do you have time to add an additional property? If not, review Chapter 9: Management Strategy and consider hiring an in-house or third-party manager. While this will be an additional cost, it could be worth it if the cash flow of the new property exceeds the fees paid to the manager.

Experience

Do you have the experience to purchase another property? If you have yet to learn and fully implement the systems and tactics taught in this book, you should spend more time implementing them with your current portfolio before purchasing another property. Scaling when you haven't perfected the operations of the properties you own will lead to bigger problems. Getting everything implemented and perfected while you have few properties is much easier than when you own more.

Data-Supported Scaling

Once again, let's return the discussion to the data. Collecting data for the exercises mentioned previously in the book has been tricky, as it relied on finding and trusting outside sources. Once you have at least one property, you can start using your own data to make decisions.

Gathering, organizing, and interpreting data is a critical step missed by most new investors that keeps them from healthily scaling, as good data is needed to make informed decisions.

Initially, if you are doing all the acquisitions and managing yourself, it is very easy to maintain your portfolio without data. As you analyze deals, find new residents, and manage existing residents, you naturally get a feel for how the business is running. You know if the market is treating buyers well or not, if rents are trending up or down, if rooms are filling slowly or quickly, all because you are in the weeds of your business every day. When you have more properties, are in more markets, and hire more team members to help you, you will lose this personal involvement in every piece of the business and thus lack the insight to make the best decisions for the company.

While you can look at many metrics for your business, two are very important to investigate before purchasing another property.

OCCUPANCY

Occupancy and vacancy are related metrics. Thus far, as part of analyzing properties, we've talked about vacancy: how much of the property is not being rented. Occupancy is the opposite of that: how much of the property is being rented. It is calculated as:

$$\text{Occupancy} = \frac{\text{Active Residents}}{\text{Units Owned}} = 1 - \text{Vacancy}$$

The goal, of course, is to keep your occupancy as high as possible, because the more residents you have, the more income you have. The issue is that as you add more units (rooms) to your portfolio, the number of residents in those rooms usually lags behind a bit, hurting your occupancy temporarily.

In Figure 16, you can see the number of units I own, the number of residents, and the occupancy over time. From zero to twenty units, things seemed to be going pretty well. I slowly acquired more units and filled them up with residents at a similar pace. At that twenty-unit mark, I achieved almost 100 percent occupancy. I was stoked! Then, a couple of things went wrong all at once, causing my occupancy to drop from nearly 100 percent to 70 percent!

Occupancy

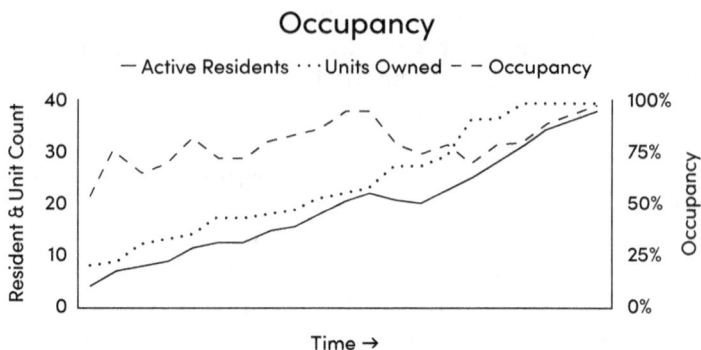

Figure 16. Occupancy for my co-living portfolio

One cause was a dip in active residents. I had just hired an in-house manager and was no longer actively involved with property management. I was not monitoring our occupancy at the time, so I had no idea rooms were becoming vacant. A few months later, I noticed my cash flow was decreasing, because my bank account balance ran low. It was not a great metric to track, as it took me months to realize there was an issue. Once I realized my in-house manager was not adequately filling the rooms, I had to temporarily step back into the management role. After some adjustments, the number of active residents started to climb again.

The second cause was that I was purchasing properties too fast, acquiring twenty more rooms over a short period. This was a problem that was more difficult to fix. While it was relatively simple to fix the management issue promptly, the number of units coming online was set in stone, as I'd already purchased the properties and was building more rooms. Sure, I could have sold the properties I had recently purchased, but after selling fees, I would lose a lot of money. The best course of action was to continue building the rooms as planned and not purchase any properties until my vacancy got closer to 100 percent again, which it eventually did.

Had I been reviewing my occupancy data every week, like I am recommending to you and like I do now, I would have realized much earlier that there was an issue on the management front that needed to be fixed, and I should have only purchased one property (around eight rooms) rather than three in quick succession.

This issue I experienced is precisely why finding a great third-party co-living manager is so hard. Many of them accept as many clients with as many rooms as possible, not considering how long it may take to fill all those new rooms, causing less-than-ideal occupancy across every investor's portfolio.

Before purchasing another property, ensure your occupancy is acceptable—probably higher than 90 percent.

RESIDENT GROWTH RATE

If you've recently acquired properties, another important metric to evaluate before purchasing another is your active resident growth rate, which measures how quickly your number of residents grows. If you haven't acquired a new property in a while, your growth rate will appear stagnant if all your rooms are filled. This is not because demand isn't there but because you've hit the limit of available rooms. In this case, the lack of growth is artificially capped, so you won't want to consider it when deciding to scale. Instead, consider reviewing interest forms from previous vacancies to gauge demand. While this isn't as precise of a measurement, it can still provide valuable insights.

To determine the resident growth rate for your portfolio, you'll need to create a graph similar to Figure 16 for your portfolio. Visually inspect it to see if the number of residents flattens or shrinks at any point in recent history.

In Figure 16, describing my portfolio, you can see that the number of residents increased over every period, except for the dip in the middle of the plot. This is a negative resident growth rate indicating that either there is a management issue preventing rooms from being filled or there are too many rooms being offered in the market for the number of residents searching (oversupply).

In either case, you should not scale until the management issue is fixed, supply has fallen, or demand has risen.

Chapter 16

More Deals

If you've decided that you are ready to scale your co-living portfolio, you still might be lacking in either deals, money, or both. This chapter will focus on increasing your deal flow by doubling down on your current market or expanding to new markets.

Double Down on Your Market

When purchasing another property, the first option is to buy within your current market. The acquisition process detailed in Part II: Buying a Co-Living Property is very scalable, so you can take that same approach again when looking for the next property. If you aren't finding deals quickly enough you'll need to put more leads at the top of the funnel.

Your first option is to open your filters to other areas of town. To decide which parts of the city to consider, repeat the room rental demand test described in Chapter 3: Selecting a Market.

Alternatively, if you used the form I provided for the test you performed earlier, you'll notice a question asking which other parts of town the applicant would consider living in. You can use this data to determine which neighborhoods have demand for co-living. If it has been a while since you performed the original room rental demand test, you may want to perform it again anyway to have newer data.

Another place where you can gather data is from your current residents. By sending them a form asking which parts of town they'd like to live in, you can incorporate this into your decision too. If you aren't getting many responses, you can incentivize them by offering $10 off their next rent payment if they fill out the form.

The other option to increase your deal flow while staying in the area of town you already operate in is to add off-market leads to your funnel. Rather than only considering on-market leads listed on the MLS, you can market directly to property owners before they list on the market. I am not an expert on this topic, as it is a whole other skill set. Personally, I've only purchased on market, but if this sounds interesting, I'd recommend reading *Real Estate Deal Maker* by Henry Washington (www.BiggerPockets.com/ReadDealMaker), as he is an expert in off-market deal finding.

Expand to Another Market

Expanding to another market is another way to increase the number of deals you can find. I recommend looking in your current market concurrently if your properties there perform well.

Adding a new market increases the complexity of your business compared to growing within your current market. You'll have to build another team (agent, lender, property manager, cleaner, repair person, etc.) and learn the ins and outs of this new market, but there are some benefits to serving another market.

First, you diversify your portfolio by serving a city that can react differently in downturns and building your income with residents working in different industries, thereby reducing the risk of losses in challenging financial times.

Second, by adding another market, you are increasing the supply of potential residents. If you double down in your current market, you add rooms to your portfolio, but the number of residents looking for a room stays fixed. Instead, you still add rooms to your portfolio by buying in a new market, but you also serve a new pool of potential residents, decreasing the risk of oversaturating your markets with rooms.

The difficulty of expanding to a new market is that some resources work well when shared across locations, but some do not.

The software and remote team members you use should work well across markets. These team members include your in-house manager (if they are virtual) and potentially your lender, insurance agent, and tax professional if they are licensed in the state of the new market.

Even if the real estate agent in your current market is licensed in the new market, I wouldn't recommend using them. To have the best outcome, you'll want to use an agent with specialized knowledge about the areas of town, industries, current listings, and more. Rarely is this the case unless the agent lives in the market themself.

If your lender, insurance agent, and tax professional aren't located in the new market, you might still be able to use them if they are licensed, but you may consider finding new team members for their specialized knowledge. Also, you'll need to find new cleaners, contractors, and repair professionals.

The systems and processes you developed might require some tweaks. For example, if your first market was in the Sunbelt, you've never had to worry about procedures regarding snow removal. If your next market is a northern market, you'll have to build those procedures out. Additionally, your acquisitions and operations may change a bit if the target resident in the new market is different. In that case, the expected stay length and room type (furnished or unfurnished) may differ. Additionally, the marketing could change if the residents in the new market prefer different listing platforms.

If you see the value in serving a new market, understand the risks, and are willing to commit time to building parts of a new team, then you'll need to select the new market. Perhaps when you first worked through Chapter 3: Selecting a Market, there was another market you found suitable. If not, you'll want to go through the selection process again from the beginning.

Chapter 17

More Money

When you have enough deals but lack the funding to purchase them, you can either wait until you've saved enough money, or you might want to partner with others willing to bring capital to the acquisition.

For any real estate partnership to succeed, you need experience, a deal, and capital. One person can bring all three pieces, or two to three people can work together and collectively bring the pieces. At this point, you know how to find deals and have the knowledge to execute the co-living strategy, but I want to emphasize the distinction between *knowledge* and *experience*. Experience is knowing a strategy, having taken action with that strategy, and having proven success. By this definition, you cannot have a successful partnership if you have not purchased and operated co-living properties multiple times with proven success on your own. It's not enough to just know what the co-living strategy is.

Asking someone for capital is not for beginners. It is an extreme responsibility that should not be taken unless you have proven you can use the co-living strategy to produce the promised returns.

Private Money Lender vs. Equity Partner

When you are looking for someone to contribute money to help fund your deals, that person can either be a private money lender or an equity partner.

A private money lender is an individual who is not given any ownership of the property. Instead, they loan you money that they expect to be paid back over time, with interest. As with any loan, the private money lender places a lien on the property, meaning that if you fail to pay them back, they have the right to take ownership of the property from you. The terms of the private money loan can be anything that the two of you decide on, but here is a typical example. A private money lender may loan you $500,000 to purchase and renovate a property. In return, they could ask you to make 10 percent interest-only payments for a three-year term. After that term, the entire $500,000 principal must be repaid.

Equity partners, conversely, can contribute capital to the deal and are given a piece of property ownership in exchange. They can have decision-making power and receive a portion of the cash flow, proceeds from the property sale, and tax benefits. If the property does not perform as expected, they share in the downside by bringing more money to the deal if cash flow is insufficient or if the property is sold for a loss.

For example, an equity partner may provide $500,000 to purchase a property while you agree to find and operate the deal. In exchange, they may have 50 percent ownership and be entitled to half of the cash flow and half of the proceeds upon sale.

While obtaining a private money loan, paying it down aggressively over a few years, and keeping 100 percent of the ownership would be great, private money loans aren't usually the best route for longer-term investments like co-living.

Since private money lenders usually want the loan to be paid back in five years or less, they are best suited for shorter-term projects like flips, where you use the capital to purchase, rehab, and then sell the property for a profit, paying the lender back their initial capital and interest within a short period. You may think that if you got a typical loan to cover most of the purchase and a private loan to cover the down payment, you could purchase a property without any of your own money. Props to you for the creative thinking, but unfortunately, this isn't allowed often. First, the first lender providing most of the funds usually has restrictions requiring that the down payment be paid directly by the buyer. Second, even if the bank allows a second lender to make the down payment, most private money lenders are unlikely to do so. In this scenario, a private money lender would have a second-position lien, meaning that if the deal goes sideways, the first lender gets paid back before the second, and they may not see the full return of their investment.

One scenario where private money loans are useful for co-living is with the buy-rehab-rent-refinance-repeat (BRRRR) method. This is best described in *Buy, Rehab, Rent, Refinance, Repeat* by David Greene (www.BiggerPockets.com/ReadBRRRR). In a nutshell, BRRRR is when you buy a very distressed property, add a lot of value through a heavy remodel, and then rent it out. For this scenario, you could purchase the property with a private money loan and no other lenders. Then, you could renovate the property, add value, and refinance it with a typical lender. With the proceeds from the refinance, you could pay off the private money loan and use the rest as the down payment on the new loan. This is a strategy for investors with a proven skill set of marketing for distressed deals and managing remodels.

More commonly, though, equity partners are a better option for purchasing co-living properties when you have limited capital. Equity partners are willing to commit to a longer-term strategy mainly because they share the deal's upside. Over time, cash flow and property value usually improve, providing generous returns to the partner.

Finding Potential Partners

The best way to find partners is to search within your friends and family, and then the friends and family of your friends and family, and then the friends and family of your friends and family of your friends and family. This looks silly when written out, but it is true.

Partnerships are built on trust. This trust is either formed directly between you and the potential partner or established because the potential partner knows someone who trusts you, so start with your friends and family. Once you have a successful partnership with one of them, your reputation will be established, and word will spread to the next layer of friends and family. As long as you continue tapping these layers, executing your responsibilities well, and being honest, you should have no shortage of potential partners.

While you can find the deal first and the partners second, I'd recommend working on the front end to create a list of potential partners first. I have done the process in reverse, and it can be really stressful to frantically search for a partner once you are under contract and have imminent deadlines.

The first partnership I formed was with a friend I'd already built trust with. It was someone I had met a couple of years prior. We were in a real estate mastermind group together and stayed in touch. Eventually, when I had gained enough experience to consider bringing in partners, I broached the idea, and he agreed to join me. Another of my partners was my lender's brother, the family of a friend. Finding partners doesn't have to be overcomplicated; just focus on the layers of friends and family.

When searching for partners, it's important to understand the legal implications of their involvement. If a partner's role is primarily passive—meaning they contribute capital but are not actively involved in the business—the partnership may be classified as a securities offering under the United States Securities and Exchange Commission (SEC). Consult an attorney to ensure the partnership structure adheres to securities regulations.

Vetting Potential Partners

Just because you know someone who may want to partner doesn't mean that you are a right fit for each other. Before purchasing a property together, you will go through phases, increasing confidence in each other or screening each other out at each step.

The first step is to just introduce the idea. At this stage, you may casually see them at an event, give them a phone call, or shoot them a text. This interaction is not a sales pitch at all; instead, it is just a regular interaction, but make sure that by the end, they know what you do in real estate, how passionate you are about it, that you've been successful thus far, and that you are looking to expand with partners.

At this stage, you don't even have to ask them if they want to partner, if you are uncomfortable. If they are interested, they will likely say so.

Once someone shows interest, you'll want to have a follow-up conversation. I'd recommend a visual discussion (not a phone call, text, or email). This can be local, at a coffee shop, or an online video call. Regardless, once again, you aren't giving them a super-hard sales pitch. Instead, you are having a more focused conversation where you:

- Further describe your investment strategy and convey your experience and success by describing examples of previous partnerships or deals you have done yourself.
- Discuss what each of you brings (experience, a deal, and/ or capital) and see if a partnership would be mutually beneficial.
- Confirm that you have similar goals for the future that this partnership helps enable.

I usually have slides to present alongside this follow-up conversation. However, it sometimes develops into a natural discussion instead. Then, I email them the slides with all the details afterward for their review.

At the end of this follow-up, determine that they still have interest by asking: How much money do you have to invest? How soon do you want to invest?

If they say that they aren't interested, no worries! There are other fish in the sea. It is not worth forcing a partnership, as it will just lead to problems down the road.

If they answer the questions and seem interested, add them to a list. You can send any future partnership opportunities to this list, and if you already have a deal you are working on, you can go ahead and give them the details then.

How many partners should you have for a deal? It just depends. I always try to have the lowest number of partners on a deal as possible to simplify everything. But I don't mind having three or four partners, as long as everyone brings something valuable.

You can learn more about real estate partnerships in *Real Estate Partnerships: How to Access More Cash, Acquire Bigger Deals, and Achieve Higher Profits* by Ashley Kehr and Tony Robinson (www.BiggerPockets.com/ReadPartnerships).

Identify the Deal

Now that you have a list of potential partners, find that next deal and present the details to those you think are best suited for the partnership. You'll want to show it to more potential partners than you need, because many who have indicated interest may not be ready to partner when it comes time to pull the trigger.

When you present the deal, should you already be under contract or discuss every offer before making it? Since I am confident in my knowledge, experience, and ability to analyze, I make offers without talking to potential partners. This saves everyone time, since chatting about every offer, when most don't get accepted, is a waste. Once under contract, I contact the partners on my list and choose the best-suited one(s). Once I have a good idea of who the partner or partners will be, we'll discuss the specifics of the partnership.

Defining the Partnership

At this point, you should discuss all the options regarding structure, responsibilities, and returns to find a combination of details that works for everyone. Once you decide how to treat each of these key points, you'll draft an operating agreement (for an LLC) or a tenancy in common agreement (for TIC) and sign it. Since you're dealing with hundreds of thousands of dollars and the future of your partners, you'll want to include a lawyer in the drafting.

Structure

Two standard partnership structures exist: a limited liability company (LLC) or tenancy in common (TIC).

LIMITED LIABILITY COMPANY

An LLC is a legal entity that you and your partner can be members of, and it's listed on the title as the property owner.

A benefit of an LLC is that it provides liability protection if handled correctly, preventing any lawsuits against the LLC from accessing your and your partner's personal assets. An operating agreement governs the LLC. Operating agreements are flexible and allow you to split the returns in many ways. Unfortunately, an LLC requires start-up and maintenance costs, such as annual filing fees and separate tax returns. Also, conventional loans do not lend to LLCs, while other programs like DSCR prefer them. Getting a traditional loan in your personal names and then transferring the title to an LLC after closing is possible and even common. However, this does incur some risk of the loan being called due for violating the due-on-sale clause.

TENANCY IN COMMON (TIC)

TIC is a method of taking ownership where the title lists each partner.

A downside of a TIC is that there is no liability protection as the LLC has, meaning that if someone sues, they can access your and your partner's assets. Also, each owner can sell their portion of the property without the consent of the other owners. A benefit is that they are cheaper than LLCs, as there are no start-up fees, and each owner reports their share of income, expenses, and depreciation on their tax returns. Also, loans like conventional loans can lend to TIC structures, while DSCR may not, depending on the lender. A TIC agreement governs the TIC and does not allow you to split the returns flexibly.

Responsibilities

Once you have agreed on a structure, you'll need to agree on the responsibilities. Some responsibilities are more intensive during the acquisition phase, and some are required for the entirety of the ownership, so you'll both want to think critically about what responsibilities you agree to accept. While you could divide responsibility in many ways, I think of them in these categories:

- Finding the deal
- Securing the deal (build the team, monitor closing actions like inspections and appraisals)
- Financing the deal
- Capital contribution
- Remodel and property setup
- Managing residents
- Bookkeeping
- Making large decisions

Returns
Next, you'll want to determine how the returns are split. I consider the returns to be in three categories.
- Cash flow: Ongoing income generated by the property after covering operating expenses, debt service, and reserves
- Appreciation: The increase in the property's value over time, realized through a sale or refinance
- Tax benefits: Deductions such as depreciation, mortgage interest, and expenses, which reduce taxable income

In a TIC structure, returns are fixed and directly tied to ownership percentages as negotiated, agreed upon, and documented on the deed and in the TIC agreement. Cash flow, appreciation, and tax benefits must be divided according to these percentages, leaving no room for customization. For example, if one partner owns 70 percent and the other owns 30 percent, all returns are split accordingly.

On the other hand, LLCs allow you to split the returns in many ways. For example, you may be in the early stages of achieving financial independence and take 70 percent of the cash flow, while the partner may have lots of active income and take 90 percent of the tax benefits to shield their income.

The exact splits you decide will mostly depend on the responsibilities you each inherit. There are no precise rules for how much each responsibility is worth. For example, as an investor bringing the deal and an expert at the strategy, I usually get 50 percent of each category while my partner gets 50 percent. In the earlier stages, when you are experienced but not an expert, you may have to offer a higher split to the other investor, as they incur more risk.

Lastly, you will want to consider how the initial capital contribution is treated.

With LLCs, you can be pretty flexible. One option is for the partners who contributed capital to receive 100 percent of the returns until paid back, and then non-capital-contributing partners begin to receive profits too. Another is for all partners to split the cash flow continually until, upon the property sale or cash-out refinance, the initial capital is returned to the contributing partners, and any proceeds beyond that are split among all partners. This has been my preferred method, providing me with a portion of the cash flow and tax benefits while incentivizing me to perform my responsibilities. Meanwhile, the capital-contributing partner receives cash flow and tax benefits and is secure in knowing they have the priority returns of their initial investment. You can treat the initial capital in many other ways, so get creative and find an option everyone agrees with.

With TICs, the returns are again fixed to the ownership amounts, so you cannot be creative with how the initial investment is returned. You cannot prioritize cash flow, appreciation, or tax benefits to help pay back the initial investment to a capital partner in an accelerated manner. For this reason, I prefer the flexibility of an LLC, especially when one partner contributes less or no capital.

Form the Partnership and Get to Work

Now that you and your partner have agreed on the terms of the partnership, you'll need to officially form your entity if you will take title in an LLC. You must file for the creation based on your state's requirements. Some online services assist with this, or you can hire a lawyer. If you take the title TIC, there is no need to form an entity.

If you are already under contract on a great deal, you can amend the purchase agreement into the name of your LLC or add your partner to the agreement if you are using TIC.

The prep work is now finished, and it is time to get to work. Moving forward, each of you will fulfill the responsibilities you've agreed to, hopefully earning massive returns for everyone along the way.

Part VI

The Co-Living Endgame

Chapter 18

Exit Strategies

While building your co-living portfolio is impactful and finan-cially fruitful, there will inevitably be a time when you need to move on from the strategy, whether that means switching to another strategy or selling some of your properties.

Switching Strategies

I am obviously a big proponent of co-living, but it could be appropriate to switch a property to another strategy at some point.

As we discussed way back in Chapter 2: Enhanced Cash Flow Strategy Comparisons (LTR, STR, MTR, Co-Living), there are pros and cons to every strategy. In the future, your goals might change from chasing every last dollar with the co-living or STR strategy to reducing management intensity in favor of less cash flow. In that case, you may switch your property to an LTR. In this hypothetical, there is a bit of work to do. First, conventional, long-term rentals are not furnished, so you must remove all the furnishings by selling or donating them. Then, you might have to undo some of the remodel-ing you performed. Improvements you made, like expanding a half bathroom by adding a shower and finishing a basement to add extra living space, are valuable to a buyer; however, some modifications to turn extra family rooms and dining rooms into bedrooms may be undone to increase the desirability. This will be much easier than constructing them, as you'll just be tearing down some framing and sheetrock, patching holes, and repainting.

Alternatively, you may decide to convert the property into an MTR or STR if conditions in the city change. Perhaps a hospital is built next to one of your properties that plans to meet its workforce demand with high-paid traveling nurses for the first few years. In this case, maybe dividing a large property into main and basement studio units would yield the best cash flow. In this case, you already have all the furnishings, but you may need to undo some conversions and line up all your room leases to expire around the same time.

Selling

Even more likely than switching to another strategy, there will come a time when it is opportune to sell one or more of your co-living properties, retire off the proceeds, purchase more single-family properties in another area, or trade into commercial assets.

When you decide to sell, you'll need to consider the residents staying in the property. While this isn't very common right now because co-living is in its infancy, in the future, it will be possible to sell the property in its current configuration to another co-living investor. This would require the least amount of work, as you wouldn't have to undo any of the remodeling and wouldn't have to remove any residents. Alternatively, you could sell it to traditional buyers, who typically drive higher demand and are willing to pay the highest price. The tricky part is that all residents must move out before the sale. To minimize lost rent, the best approach is to plan the sale at least a year in advance and align all new lease end dates around the anticipated sale date. Once vacant, you could remove the furnishings and undo some conversions as you would if converting to the LTR strategy.

Chapter 19

The Co-Living Legacy

Congratulations! You are now equipped to be an expert at buying, remodeling, furnishing, and managing co-living properties! With housing becoming unaffordable for many, thank you for being part of the solution.

By using the systems and knowledge in this book, you aren't simply providing an affordable housing option. You are taking a community-first approach that will enrich the lives of those you serve.

As you build your co-living portfolio, get excited knowing that you are one of the founding members of the strategy. As time marches on and rental affordability remains an issue, continue to execute the plan with your communities in mind, setting an example for future investors who adopt the strategy.

Remember that this is not a set-it-and-forget-it strategy. Since it is in its infancy, improved practices will continue to be uncovered. Stay educated and survey your communities often, making improvements to elevate the experience for your residents.

Along with the good you are doing for the world, I hope you enjoy all the cash flow this strategy can provide. May it help you reach your goal, whether it is supplementing your current income, preparing you for traditional retirement, or retiring you from your job now.

You are pioneering a movement that reimagines housing, bringing comfort and security to residents while generating incredible financial returns. Keep your values at the heart of your business, embrace growth, and celebrate the impact you're making in the lives of others and your own. Here's to building a future where housing is accessible, community centered, and rewarding for everyone involved. The best is yet to come.

And remember, it's not rocket science; it's just real estate.

Acknowledgments

To my extraordinary wife, Elijah: You bring me back to earth when I need to refocus, yet you encourage me to fly higher when I doubt my abilities. I'm inspired by your strength and grateful for your motivation.

About the Author

Miller McSwain is a former nuclear rocket scientist turned real estate industry expert. Based in Colorado Springs, Miller and his wife have built a thriving co-living portfolio, managing six properties with forty-one rooms alongside partners. Known for his innovative approach and deep knowledge of the co-living strategy, Miller helps others maximize rental income, streamline operations, and achieve financial independence.

BiggerPockets ®

BiggerPockets Rental Property Calculator

www.BiggerPockets.com/BookRPC

BiggerPockets Deal Finder

www.BiggerPockets.com/BookDeals

BiggerPockets Market Finder

www.BiggerPockets.com/BookMarkets

BiggerPockets Agent Finder

www.BiggerPockets.com/BookAgent

BiggerPockets Lender Finder

www.BiggerPockets.com/BookLender

BiggerPockets Property Management Finder

www.BiggerPockets.com/BookPM

Reference List

Apartment List Research Team. "Apartment List National Rent Report." Apartment List. March 2, 2025. https://www.apartmentlist.com/research/national-rent-data.

"Changes in Basic Minimum Wages in Non-Farm Employment Under State Law: Selected Years 1968 to 2024." U.S. Department of Labor. Accessed January 15, 2025. https://www.dol.gov/agencies/whd/state/minimum-wage/history.

Ferris, Tim. *The 4-Hour Workweek: Escape 9-5, Live Anywhere, and Join the New Rich.* Harmony Books, 2009.

McMullen, Laura. "How Much Should I Spend on Rent?" NerdWallet. December 9, 2024. https://www.nerdwallet.com/article/finance/how-much-should-i-spend-on-rent.

"Median Personal Income in the United States." FRED: Federal Reserve Bank of St. Louis. Updated September 10, 2024. https://fred.stlouisfed.org/series/MEPAINUSA646N.

"Reasonable Accommodations and Modifications." U.S. Department of Housing and Urban Development. Accessed January 15, 2025. https://www.hud.gov/program_offices/fair_housing_equal_opp/reasonable_accommodations_and_modifications.

SUPERCHARGE YOUR REAL ESTATE INVESTING.

Get **exclusive bonus content** like checklists, contracts, interviews, and more when you buy from the BiggerPockets Bookstore.

Use code **FirstBPBook** for **15%** off your first purchase.

Standard shipping is free and you get bonus content with every order!

www.BiggerPockets.com/STORE

BiggerPockets Newsletter Signup

Want access to more content? Sign up for the BiggerPockets Newsletter using the QR Code below. Covering a range of current topics of conversation, keep in the know about investing in your area.

Sign up now.
www.BiggerPockets.com/newsletter

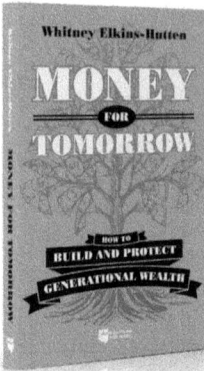

Money for Tomorrow: How to Build and Protect Generational Wealth by Whitney Elkins-Hutten

Money comes and goes, but your wealth legacy will endure for generations—and winning the multigenerational wealth game means understanding the rules of play.

www.BiggerPockets.com/ ReadMoneyForTomorrow

Real Estate by the Numbers: A Complete Reference Guide to Deal Analysis by J Scott and Dave Meyer

From cash flow to compound interest, *Real Estate by the Numbers* makes it easy for anyone to master real estate deal analysis.

www.BiggerPockets.com/ ReadBytheNumbers

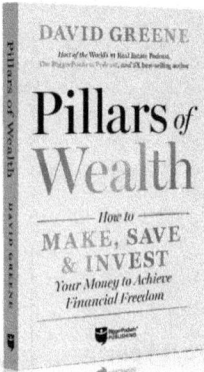

Pillars of Wealth: How to Make, Save, and Invest Your Money to Achieve Financial Freedom by David Greene

Take the guesswork out of financial freedom with a strategy perfected by countless self-made millionaires.

www.BiggerPockets.com/ReadPillars

Set for Life, Revised Edition: An All-Out Approach to Early Financial Freedom by Scott Trench

Retire early from your nine-to-five and reach financial freedom with the actionable advice in this personal finance best-seller with more than 130,000 copies sold.

www.BiggerPockets.com/ReadSetForLife

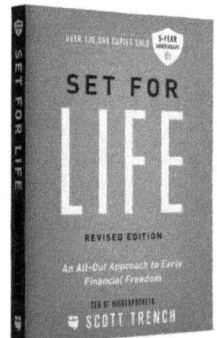

Looking for more?
Join the BiggerPockets Community

BiggerPockets brings together education, tools, and a community of more than 3 million+ like-minded members—all in one place. Learn about investment strategies, analyze properties, connect with investor-friendly agents, and more.

Go to **biggerpockets.com** to learn more!

Listen to a **BiggerPockets Podcast**

Watch **BiggerPockets on YouTube**

Join the **Community Forum**

Learn more on **the Blog**

Read more **BiggerPockets Books**

Learn about our **Real Estate Investing Bootcamps**

Connect with an **Investor-Friendly Real Estate Agent**

Go Pro! Start, scale, and manage your portfolio with your **Pro Membership**

Follow us on social media!

Join over 3 million investors on BiggerPockets forums. Whether you're a seasoned expert or just starting out, tap into the collective knowledge, confidence, and connections to reach your full potential.

Join the conversation now!
BiggerPockets.com/BookForums

BiggerPockets®